# Live Like
## *a Hot Chick*

Also by Jodi Lipper and Cerina Vincent

HOW TO EAT LIKE A HOT CHICK
HOW TO LOVE LIKE A HOT CHICK

# Live Like
## *a Hot Chick*

### How to Feel Sexy, Find Confidence, and Create Balance at Work and Play

## Jodi Lipper and Cerina Vincent

**AVON**

*An Imprint of* HarperCollins*Publishers*

This book is obviously not meant to replace the care or advice of a medical or other healthcare professional. We think that you should always consult with a real doctor before making any radical changes to your eating or fitness habits. Please take care of yourselves! We are not responsible if you take us too seriously and get yourself sick or injured. And if you're under eighteen, ask your mom if you should be reading this!

HarperCollins books may be purchased for educational, business, or sales promotional use. For information please write: Special Markets Department, HarperCollins Publishers, 10 East 53rd Street, New York, NY 10022.

FIRST AVON PAPERBACK EDITION PUBLISHED 2010.

*Based on the design by Reshma Chattaram Chamberlin*

Library of Congress Cataloging-in-Publication Data
   Lipper, Jodi.
     Live like a hot chick : how to feel sexy, find confidence, and create balance at work and play / by Jodi Lipper, Cerina Vincent.
       p.  cm.
     Includes bibliographical references and index.
     ISBN 978-0-06-195907-3 (pbk.)
     1. Women—Psychology.   2. Self-esteem in women.   3. Women—Conduct of life.   4. Life skills.   5. Success.   I. Vincent, Cerina.
     II. Title.
   HQ1206.L547 2010
   646.70082—dc22                       2010015005

10 11 12 13 14  OV/RRD  10 9 8 7 6 5 4 3 2 1

*For every woman who longs to feel beautiful,*
*inspired, and fully in control of her life.*

# **Contents**

**Hot Chick** *(definition):* A confident woman. She knows what she wants and gets it. She is aware of her flaws, but she doesn't obsess over them and instead thinks that maybe (just maybe) they actually add to her unique beauty. She is passionate. She loves life. She is comfortable in her own skin and owns her sexuality, but uses it purely for good. She does not see other women as her enemy and competes only with herself to do her best at all times and to be her best at all times. She is forthright, honest, and disarmingly herself. She is having fun, and she is sexy, and you just want to be around her to soak up some of those good vibes. She isn't perfect, but she doesn't care because she is hot. And so are you.

# *Introduction*

## How Do I Live Like a Hot Chick?

KNOWING THAT YOU ARE A HOT CHICK (BY OUR DEF-
INITION) IS TRULY THE FIRST STEP TO LIVING LIKE
ONE. If you don't fully believe it yet, that's okay. So many of us
spend so much time working our hot asses off to make ends meet
that we don't have one second left at night to appreciate the fact
that our asses are, in fact, hot. Who has the time nowadays to
consciously work on becoming more confident and empowered,
or to tell herself that she's beautiful? We want you to know that
we've been there, and you know what? We're still there right along
with you. Through our friendship, we helped each other get over
our own food and body image issues and stop being LSE♥ about
dating so that we could indulge without guilt and find the love of
our lives, and we wrote our first two books, *How to Eat Like a Hot
Chick* and *How to Love Like a Hot Chick*, so that we could share

---

♥    Every time you see one of these, flip to the Hot Lingo section for the
definition.

that life-changing advice with all of you. But we still have to fight to stay inspired and positive about work when we're stressed out about money, to find time for the important things in life like friends, family, and love, and of course to always feel like confident Hot Chicks deep down inside. Finding balance in our lives is a constant work in progress, but just like our struggles with food and love, we are helping each other through it—and we are going to help you, too.

It doesn't matter if you are just out of high school, starting to work your way up in the world, or a single mom who's juggling twelve hats; we want you to know that you are a Hot Chick who deserves to feel that way in every aspect of your life. No matter how old you are, what size jeans you wear, or what you do for a living it sometimes feels impossible to find a happy balance between work and play in this crazy, stressful world. We do consider ourselves feminists, but sometimes we wonder if parts of the feminist movement have really screwed us over. Of course it's great that we can demand equal pay and equal rights, lead major companies, and run for president—but is it possible that we've taken on too much? Nowadays, not only *can* we do it all, but women are *pressured* to do it all, all the time, and to look flawless while doing it.

Too many of us are expected to work twelve-hour days to bring home the bacon, fry it up, do the laundry, pay the bills, pop out babies, raise the babies, take the lead in our relationships when it comes to finances, and simultaneously try to somehow feel beautiful and sassy enough to keep our relationships hot and steamy. We almost never find time to nurture the important relationships with our girlfriends or even ourselves, and if we ever magically find five seconds to relax and flip through a magazine, we're faced with airbrushed, Botoxed, fake-tanned celebrities who represent a completely unrealistic ideal of beauty that none of us totally agree with—but that still makes us feel bad about ourselves. It's no wonder why so many of us are running around feeling crazed and LSE♥ with critical cases of OWL Syndrome♥.

There are other women who have the opposite problem— who aren't doing much of anything at all because they're so un-inspired, negative, full of complaints, and busy acting like spoiled fifteen-year-olds who think that their lives suck and that it just isn't fair. If this is you (and you know who you are), and you believe that your life would be better in someone else's four-inch shoes, not only are you wrong, but you are fucking up♥ by fail-ing to appreciate everything that you already have. You have so much to be grateful for; if you can't think of anything right now, be grateful that you have eyes and can read this book, because we are going to give you a fresh and inspiring perspective while teaching you how to truly appreciate and enjoy every moment of the life you are lucky enough to have.

We've broken this book down into three sections to help you start living every part of your life like the Hot Chick that you are. First is "How to Feel Like a Hot Chick," because you can't live, act, or even look like a Hot Chick if your soul isn't brimming over with confidence and positive vibes. Second comes "How to Work Like a Hot Chick," which will help you act like a super savvy Hot Chick on the job and tell you how to do your job with so much powerful poise that you'll stay sane, become motivated, and stop dreading Mondays quite so much. Finally, we're going to teach you "How to Play Like a Hot Chick," because you can't have a balanced, beautiful, and truly meaningful life if you don't take time to relax, explore the world, celebrate this one and only life of yours, and nurture your relationships with the people you choose to spend it with.

Life is hard but it's also short, and we've all got to stop wast-ing time hating our beautiful, womanly bodies and stressing about work, money, and just not being good enough. It's time to strike a healthy balance so that we can feel secure and encouraged and actually start enjoying our lives. This is your one and only heyday♥, and if you waste it covering up at the beach, playing small♥, and ignoring all of the juicy, magic♥ moments that life has to offer, we know that you will look back and regret it. You deserve a life that is as rewarding and fulfilling as it is challenging, and in this book we are going to show you—finally!—how you can have it all.

How would it feel to be financially secure, sure of yourself, and soul-satisfied? Have you stopped wondering what that would be like because it seems like an impossible goal? Well, by the time we're done with you, you'll have all of the information, tools, tips, and confidence that you need to go out there and tackle the world like the feminine, sexy, empowered Hot Chick that you were meant to be. Get ready and get excited, Hot Chicks. You are on your way to looking hot, feeling hotter, and transforming the chaos of your life into the life of your dreams. Let's get started!

# Part I

## How to Feel Like a Hot Chick

BEFORE WE BEGIN, GO BACK TO THE FIRST PAGE AND REREAD EVERY WORD OF OUR DEFINITION OF A HOT CHICK. Please remember that when we talk about being hot, looking hot, or feeling hot, we are not talking about looking like you walked off the cover of an airbrushed magazine or ever remotely resembling a slutty reality TV star. We are referring to an inner hotness that is so freaking savvy and sexy that it makes you glow from the inside out. It's so irresistible that men, women, children, and even puppies are drawn to it. This is what happens when you are confident, passionate, happy, empowered, and you use all of that goodness to create a balanced life for yourself that leaves you enlightened instead of exhausted.

Before we can move on to help you find joy and contentment in your professional or personal life, we need to teach you how to feel like the Hot Chick that you are deep down in your bones.

No more comparing yourself to supermodels or even the girl next door, no more beating yourself up over cravings for ice cream, and no more dreading exercise and then hating yourself for skipping it! Get ready for the confidence makeover of a lifetime that will leave you feeling exactly as you should—like a Hot Chick.

# Chapter 1

## *Love Your Body*

WE DON'T KNOW A SINGLE HOT CHICK OUT THERE WHO WAKES UP EVERY MORNING TRULY LOVING EVERY SQUARE INCH OF HER PERFECTLY IMPERFECT BODY. Even the most technically beautiful women on the planet have days when they just can't stand to look in the mirror and weeks when they feel unfeminine and powerless and let their LSE♥ rule their lives. We are pretty sure that Angelina Jolie doesn't always feel like the super gorgeous goddess that we all see. She probably feels just like the rest of us—physically and mentally exhausted and stressed the fuck out. We're pretty sure that Angie notices new lines on her face on every birthday just like we do and little unhappy body changes with each new baby just like every other woman out there. Our point is that no matter what we look like or how much money we make, we are all comprised of the same messy, complicated female hormones that make us nurturing, compassionate, beautiful, and feminine—but at times also LSE♥, self-deprecating, competitive, depressed, and unbelievably, unfairly hard on ourselves. Sigh.

Freeing ourselves of this self-hatred is the first step towards living like a Hot Chick. How can you really be the person you want to be in your career, social life, and love life if you wake up every day hating the very body that you move through life in? We spent too many years picking apart our own flaws and assets instead of embracing them, and as a result we felt insecure and insufficient instead of empowered and competent in every part of our lives. Now we see so many women wasting their lives doing this very same thing. Every time our girlfriends get together, they immediately start complaining about their love handles, thin hair, pale skin, crow's feet, or even big feet. Too many women are blind to their own beauty, and enough is enough, Hot Chicks! It's time to transform those negative thoughts and feelings about yourself into something that will help make your life magical♥, and that (of course) is feeling like a Hot Chick, inside and out.

# The History of Beauty Is Beautiful

We saw one of the world's first known pornographic images recently and it was fascinating for so many reasons. The sketch of a naked woman sitting on a bicycle (ouch!) had saggy boobs, an equally saggy belly (complete with several rolls), and thighs that were drawn to look like they were covered in lumps of cellulite. This woman would be considered obese and unattractive today, but at one time she was the epitome of sex appeal and had men all over the world jacking off to her. (Sorry to be gross, but it's true.) It's no surprise to anyone that beauty standards have changed over time. At any museum in the world, you can literally watch them gradually morph as you walk from room to room and era to era throughout history.

Until recently, even idealized images heightened women's natural qualities, from our large, imperfect breasts and pearly skin to our dimply cellulite. But now that unnatural enhancements have crept into the mainstream, they have also infiltrated our beauty standards. We can whiten our teeth, and so ultra white teeth have become the standard; we can inject poison into our skin to deaden the nerves, and so expressionless, lineless faces have become the standard; we can lie in a tanning bed until we turn strange colors, and so year-round, tanned-as-leather skin has become the standard; we can slice up our faces and our bodies and insert bags of silicone, and so ridiculously high, large breasts that look more like beach balls than body parts have become the standard.

Somewhere in between that old pornographic image and the idealization of Hef's enhanced girlfriends, we have really done some damage. We think that one of the worst by-products of this is that today's beauty standard leaves no room for variety. While we may see more ethnic and racial diversity today than we did twenty or thirty years ago, everyone now somehow looks the same, with the same thin bodies, perfect abs, shiny veneers, dark tans, and fake boobs. It is a very strange time to be a woman when Jennifer Aniston looks just like Miley Cyrus and Alicia Keys is starting to resemble Jessica Biel. Almost every month we look at the cover of our favorite fashion magazines and wonder, *Who is that?* These gorgeous cover girls are so made up and airbrushed into conformity that we literally can't pick some of the world's most famous women out of a lineup. These women are all beautiful and we rejoice in their beauty, but we want to celebrate different types of beauty, too, from sexy flat chests and seductively round hips to the natural lines that come with wisdom, expression, and laughter.

The only way to change today's beauty ideals (or at least the way they impact our self-esteem) is for all of us women to join forces and change things for ourselves with our words and our actions. It's so easy to cut down another woman instead of complimenting her, but doing that only makes the world a less hospitable place for all of us. When you prop another woman up, refuse to see her flaws, and focus on her beauty instead, you are changing things for the better—for yourself, and for all women. You may not know it yet, but you are a Hot Chick with the power to change the world, and when you put good energy out, the universe ♥ always brings it back.

# How You Can Love Your Body

Every day you spend hating your body is a day that you are not living like a Hot Chick. Your time and energy should be spent on accomplishing your dreams and enjoying your life, not making yourself feel worthless and wallowing in self-pity. It's time to put an end to your negative, insecure thoughts and genuinely embrace the body that you have. Here's how to start.

### #1—Misery Loves Company

This actually helped us get over our own body image issues. When we first met, we both secretly eyed each other and thought, *She is so beautiful and perfect-looking; she must be completely confident and have all her shit together.* But once we became friends, we learned that we shared the exact same LSE♥ and insecurities and it taught each of us a huge lesson—that every woman you envy and admire probably feels the same way about herself that you do about yourself. If this is the case, then isn't it stupid for all of us to waste our time and energy feeling this way? Shouldn't every single one of us just stop it right now and love what we have, instead? If someone who looks like Cindy Crawford feels just as unconfident as you, isn't there very little point in wasting your life wishing that you looked like Cindy Crawford?

It may not seem like a Hot Chick concept to find happiness through someone else's pain, but don't you feel a little bit better knowing that it's not just you? You are not alone in this battle against the word's crazy idea of beauty. We and you and millions of other women all over the world feel exactly the same way: scared shitless of being seen naked in florescent lighting and pissed off that we can never truly enjoy cheesy, greasy, decadent, chocolaty food without feeling at least a little bit guilty. Misery does indeed love company, so let the fact that you are not alone with these thoughts and feelings help set you free from them.

### #2—Sweet Talk

How often do you think, *I hate myself,* or *I'm a worthless pig because I skipped the gym to eat an entire cheesecake on the couch,* or even something as minor as, *My arms look fat today; I wish I had that girl's hair and her ankles?* It's not just you; many of us talk to ourselves this way constantly, and it is destructive for each and every one of us. The more you tell yourself that you are a fat pig, the more you will feel like a fat pig—and the more likely you'll be to treat yourself like a fat pig. Then what? That's right; you will feel even more like a fat pig and start the entire process over from step one.

This is an incredibly vicious cycle that you can turn around very simply. All you have to do is change the way you talk to yourself. Every time you start to think mean thoughts, reverse them. Tell yourself that you are beautiful and powerful and a total Hot Chick who deserves to love her body. If you truly dislike something about your body, stop focusing on it and think about something you like about yourself. Remind yourself how pretty your eyes are, or how sexy your décolletage is. When you focus on the things about yourself that are beautiful, you will eventually believe that you are beautiful and start treating yourself that way, too, and a positive, productive cycle will replace the vicious one. You'll start exuding confidence instead of self-hatred, and you'll want to honor and cherish your beautiful body by taking care of it instead of treating it like shit. These little changes will add up over time, and eventually you will feel like the Hot Chick that you are.

## #3—Do Your Own Job

Are you a *Sports Illustrated* swimsuit model, or planning to be in the next Victoria's Secret fashion show? We're pretty sure that it's not your job to look perfect, so why are you comparing yourself to celebrities whose actual job it is to look flawless all the time? The women in movies and magazines really do get paid to have white teeth, a winter tan, and perfectly highlighted hair. These women also hire personal chefs, dieticians, trainers, hair and makeup artists, and stylists to help them do their job of looking good. But you probably have another job that involves using your brain, skills, and talents instead of your boobs, butt, and fake eyelashes. If your body is involved in your job, it's almost certainly to give you the strength and stamina to do it well, so cherish the fact that your body is doing its job and stop trying to make it do somebody else's! Until every supermodel out there is expected to do your job as well as you can, please stop pressuring yourself to do theirs.

## #4—List Your Loves

Now that you know how powerful your words are, we want you to put some of them down on paper and create a list of the things that you love about your body. This will help you realize right now how many wonderful traits you actually have, plus it will be something that you can look at on those LSE♥ days when you can't remember a single one of them. No playing small♥ here, girls; we are telling you to be as conceited as possible! Also, just for the moment, we want you to be superficial. If you have a huge heart and a high IQ, we hope you know how important and valuable that is—but we know that it won't necessarily make you love your body any more when the tabloids say that Jennifer Love Hewitt is too fat and you're six sizes bigger than she is. Take your time, wrack your brain, and write down all of the things about your body that you are grateful for. Remember that nobody is going to see this list but you; don't hold back, and don't focus exclusively on the things that other people find attractive. Do you secretly love the tone of your triceps or the womanly curve of your hips? Does it make you happy to see your father's imperfect nose or your grandmother's lips in the mirror? Use this space to honor your body and every beautiful part of it.

_____

_____

_____

_____

_____

_____

_____

_____

_____

_____

_____

## #5—Acknowledge and Dismiss

After all of this, are there still niggling, negative thoughts in your brain that just won't go away? That's okay; you just need to give these thoughts their proper due by acknowledging them, accepting them, and dismissing them. In order to do that, we want you to write down the things that are preventing you from fully loving and accepting your body; then add a statement about how you will no longer let them stop you from doing so. Unlike the previous exercise, we don't want you to try really hard to come up with a million negative thoughts; that would defeat the purpose. We just want you to recognize the few things that you wish you could change about yourself and tell the universe♥ on paper that you refuse to let these so-called flaws make you feel bad about yourself. For example, you can write, "It would be fun to be taller, but I love my body the way it is," or, "I wish I could lose those last ten pounds, but I won't let a measly ten pounds stop me from feeling confident and sexy," but you must not write, "I will never be happy until I lose fifty pounds." Got it? Good.

# Real Men Love Real Women

This book isn't about men; it's about you. However, our relationships with our bodies are often directly connected to our relationships with men. So many women worry about what they look like not so they can feel good about themselves, but so that they can find love and impress men. We drive ourselves crazy hoping that we are hot enough to hold their attention on a first date and then worry ourselves sick about whether or not our men will still love us when we're pregnant and swollen or wrinkled with boobs that dangle at our knees. To make matters worse, the media constantly reinforces the idea that in order to keep a man, we must remain youthful and flawless at all costs, whether that means age-preventing Botox and lip injections or post-baby boob lifts and tummy tucks.

While of course there are some men out there who want a woman like the ones they see on TV, with platinum hair extensions and Barbie's body, it is more often than not women (not men) who reinforce these false beauty standards and pressure themselves to look a certain way. Most men actually hate fake nails that might come off in their hair, high heels that turn you into a veritable cripple, tanning sprays that make you smell strangely like mashed potatoes, and especially fake breasts that don't bounce around like the ones Mother Nature made. Have you ever heard a man tell you that you're at your sexiest when you just wake up in the morning—bed head, complete lack of make-up, morning breath, and all? Well, he wasn't just saying that to get you into bed (though it didn't hurt, did it?). Men are hard wired to be attracted to women, period. Their genetic code tells them to be turned on by round hips that can carry a child and their sixth sense forces them to chase you around when you're ovulating, but there is nothing in their DNA that makes them attracted to silicone, clip-on ponytails, or botulism.

What if we all started loving our bodies and walking around with total confidence, began eating dessert without guilt, and stopped letting insecurities hold us back in the bedroom? Do you think men would rebel, stop having sex with women, and insist that we all continue to try to look like playmates—or would they love the fact that they could finally stop trying to convince us that those pants don't make our legs look like sausages, that one slice of pizza won't ruin our bodies, and that sex is actually more fun with the lights on? We are pretty damn sure it would be the latter, and we want you to remember that the next time you're on a date, with your husband, or just gabbing to your friends about how you want to lose twenty pounds so that you can finally meet a guy.

Forget that handful of BMS♥ guys who think that Heidi Montag is a goddess and trust that there are real men out there who would prefer to have you snuggled up next to them in sweat pants than dancing for them in pasties and stilettos. The next time you are tempted to complain about your love handles or wish you had your best friend's hair, stop and ask yourself why. Do you want a different body for you, or because deep down you think it will make you more desirable? If it's the latter, remind yourself that the most desirable women on the planet are not physically perfect. They may be beautiful, but it's the way they shine from the inside out that makes them so sexy. Those are the real Hot Chicks, and they are the ones who are sought after by all the real men.

# *Enhance Your Beauty*

Before we go any further, we want to take a second to address the inherent contradictions that come with talking about these body image issues. Unless you're a farmer with longer hair coming out of your armpits than on your head, it's impossible not to succumb to the pressure to conform to today's beauty standards at least a little bit. We can tell you all day long that you should feel confident in your body the way it is, but we'd be total lying bitches if we didn't admit to feeling this pressure, too—and to sometimes giving in to it. If we tell you that your natural skin is beautiful but spend ten minutes in a tanning bed before a TV appearance so that we don't look sickeningly pale on camera, does that make us frauds? And what if we take a stand against the popularity of breast implants but wear push-up bras out at night so that we feel sexy in our low-cut dresses?

Well, we think that everyone has to draw her own line in the sand when it comes to this stuff, and every woman's line might be in a slightly different place. It's kind of like religion, where even if you totally believe in G*d, the majority of people don't follow 100 percent of the rules that their particular faith dictates. We pick and choose what works for us—the potato pancakes over the head shaving, or the Christmas presents over the lack of premarital sex—and that's okay. We feel the same way about body image, so in our case we choose the bikini waxes and lip glosses over chin implants and labiaplasty (ew!)—but your choices might be different.

What truly makes you feel beautiful? If it's getting a mani/pedi on a Saturday afternoon and then sporting a pair of stripper-sized fake eyelashes that night, fine. If lazering off your arm hair makes you appreciate your soft skin, go ahead and do it. We won't judge you. In fact, we want you to do whatever you need to do in order to enhance, flaunt, and celebrate your femininity along with that beautiful body of yours. We want you to find a balance between embracing the natural body that the universe♥ gave you and doing little things that make you love it even more. The trick is to first accept yourself the way you are and *then* embrace the enhancements so that you never start believing that you need them in order to be beautiful. They're just some delicious, indulgent icing on a fabulous, delectable cake.

# Ten Things You Can Do Right Now to Feel Better About Your Body

The best way to squash any type of insecurity is to face it head on, be bold, and do things that you never thought you could do. Here is our list of acts that will help you feel brave, secure, and light-hearted about all of this heavy body image stuff. Some of them are silly and others might offend you, but stop judging and trust us that these little things are actually empowering.

### #1—Find Bikini Bliss
You might think we're crazy (and you might be right), but one great way to get comfortable in your own skin is to let it all hang out as often as you can. Try wearing fewer clothes at home when you're cooking, cleaning, or watching TV. When you keep your body covered up and think negative thoughts, you will start to believe that your body is a lot worse than it actually is. Find freedom by taking it all off and getting comfortable with your body the way it is.

### #2—Hit the Steam
Your gym's locker room, saunas, and steam rooms are great places to see the beautiful variety of women's bodies on display. Stop desperately focusing on tying your towel around your body and take a look around (discreetly, please). Notice how different and amazing our bodies all are, from the varying colors to different shapes, sizes, and dimensions. The more you see this array of bodies in the flesh, the more you'll accept and cherish your own.

### #3—Skinny Dip

Without getting hypothermia or arrested for indecent exposure, find a way to do this at least once in your life. Diving into water in your birthday suit makes you feel weightless and one with nature. You'll realize that there's no reason to cover up, suck it in, or find an angle that makes your legs look longer, because nature is perfect the way the universe ♥ made it—and so are you.

### #4—Self-Love

Yes, we mean *that*. How can you be comfortable in the bedroom with a man if you don't first get comfortable in the bedroom by yourself? The better you get to know your body, the more you will appreciate and love it for all of the amazing things that it can do. Get some fun toys, lock yourself away, and get excited about getting yourself excited. If this doesn't help you embrace your body, we honestly don't know what will.

### #5—Wax On, Wax Off

Remember that *Sex and the City* episode where Carrie got a Brazilian wax and it made her kiss Vince Vaughn? Well, if all it takes is a bikini wax to get that kind of passion and confidence running through your veins, then a bikini wax it is! We don't ever want you to feel like you have to be hairless in order to please a man, but doing something different and daring like this can help you see yourself in a different light. Why not try it? You've got nothing to lose except a little bit of hair (or maybe a lot).

### #6—Do Some Good

Nothing will make you realize how utterly ridiculous and stupid your body image issues are faster than volunteering at the children's cancer ward of a local hospital or at a retirement home. Try seeing yourself through their eyes—you are healthy and beautiful and absolutely perfect, and we really hope you can appreciate what you've got while you've got it and focus on helping these people who need it.

### #7—Slip Into Something Sexy

We know we just told you that your man loves you in a stained sweatshirt and jeans—and he does—but sometimes it's easier to love ourselves when we dress our bodies prettily. Remember the old days when women brushed their hair for an hour each night in front of a vanity mirror while wearing a silk robe? Embrace your femininity at the end of a long day by putting on something that makes you feel like a woman. Steer clear of the crotchless panties and corsets and treat yourself to a simple satin nightie that will softly embrace your curves so that you can, too!

### #8—Strip

Again, this is not about turning a man on; it's about turning yourself on to your feminine power. There are now pole-dancing classes around the country for women of every age, shape, and size, and taking one can help you learn to love the way your body moves and appreciate the strength it possesses. You'll see short, outgoing lawyers, tall, shy teachers, and heavyset accountants all learning and working together and appreciating each other's unique beauty. These classes are great exercise, but they're even better for your mind than your body.

### #9—Take up Yoga

Getting biceps like Madonna's is a fringe benefit of yoga, but the primary purpose is to create a connection between the mind and body. Yoga is actually more similar to meditation than other forms of exercise. It teaches you to move through uncomfortable positions peacefully, find calmness amidst life's chaos, and breathe through stressful situations. How can you not love your body after you've done all that? You don't meet many yogis who suffer from poor body image, so take a note from ancient India and find your inner Zen master.

### #10—Have Sex
What better way to feel all of your sexy power than to let your body experience the greatest and most natural form of pleasure? This time, though, make sure to notice how much enjoyment your body is giving someone else as well as yourself, and know that there is no other body out there that could do it better. Just please remember to be safe!

# Chapter 2

## Work It Out

WE CAN TALK ALL DAY LONG ABOUT HOW LOOKING
LIKE YOUR FAVORITE STAR WON'T ACTUALLY MAKE YOU
HAPPY, BUT THE TRUTH IS THAT IN ORDER TO GENU-
INELY FEEL LIKE A HOT CHICK INSIDE AND OUT, YOU
NEED TO TURN OFF THE TV, GET YOUR HOT ASS OFF
OF THE COUCH, AND MOVE! We can't stress to you enough
how much exercise can help you feel (and look) your best—it can
completely change the way you experience life in your skin. Hitting the gym, the pavement, or even the dance floor to get regular
exercise will change your life for the better in so many ways. It will
not only help you lose those unwanted pounds that are keeping
your from feeling like the Hot Chick that you are, but working out
will also boost your mood, elevate your energy levels, and help you
live a longer and hotter life.

Some of you may already have an exercise regimen that
totally works for you, but we know that many of you are strug-

gling with a lack of motivation, information, or even equipment. (Let's face it, if your exercise routine involves curling cans of soup or stepping on a pile of newspapers, it's not going to work.) It's time to stop wasting money on junky apparatuses that promise to give you flat abs in twelve days and supplements that will only add extra calories to your day. Instead, follow our common sense, real life advice on how to save time and money on exercise while feeling inspired, energized, and hotter than ever. Exercise not only helps you feel good physically and mentally, but it makes you feel proud of yourself for doing something good for that hot body of yours. When you are proud of yourself you feel more confident, and when you feel confident you are motivated to make smarter choices for your body. Isn't it nice to finally find a body image cycle that is healthy and productive instead of vicious and self-defeating?

# Lesser Known Magical Benefits of Exercise

Exercise will certainly change your body by burning calories, building muscle, and sweating out toxins, but it will also change your entire life for the better. Once you start to exercise with enthusiasm and begin reaping all these benefits, you'll not only enjoy it but you'll crave it almost as much as chocolate cake. (Well, kinda.) Take a look at these magical benefits of exercise and start benefitting from them now!

### Magical Benefit #1—It's More Effective than Red Bull

Exercise is the most natural energy booster on the planet (other than sex, but if you're doing it right, that *totally* counts as exercise). No matter how many nasty energy drinks you chug, how much caffeine you ingest, or how many Vitamin B supplements you choke down, nothing compares to the all-natural, completely beneficial energy boost that comes after a good workout.

### Magical Benefit #2—You Can Have Your Cake and Eat It, Too

Of course you already know that exercise burns calories, but there is really no other way than regular exercise to indulge in sweets on a regular basis without all of those muffins forming a muffin top on you. We're not saying that you have to punish yourself for eating, but think about how much extra food Michael Phelps gets to eat just because he burns it all off in the pool. Consistent exercise gives you the freedom to indulge without guilt and what girl doesn't want that?

### Magical Benefit #3—It's a Friend Finder

We've met countless friends at butt class ♥ and even met each other at the gym, so we're speaking from experience when we say there is no better time to meet true friends than when you're sweating profusely, stinky, and gasping for air. If the girl on the next bike is happy to see you like that, then she'll really like you after a shower and a martini.

### Magical Benefit #4—It's a Break for Your Brain

All of us poor Hot Chicks today run around juggling nine thousand different things and by the end of the day, we're maxed out and mentally spent. Our brains are always spinning, trying to make sure we remember to schedule a pap spear, get an oil change—and not mix up the two! Sure, watching reality TV is a great way to zone out and quiet the incessant brain chatter, but exercise does all of that while making your muscles, heart, and lungs do the work instead of your brain. When you let your body make all of the decisions for a while, you'll walk away with tighter muscles and a calmer mind.

### Magical Benefit #5—You Might Meet a Cute Boy . . .

. . . or girl (we don't discriminate)! If you're spending hours looking for dates online or in bars, get yourself to the gym, a group hike, or a local softball league and look around for someone interesting there. You might find true love while giving your heart and bod the chance to get double the exercise with some sweaty, post-workout action.

### Magical Benefit #6—Take Time for You

We all need more "me time," and working out is the best way to make use of that time to yourself. It's nearly as meditative as meditation, almost as relaxing as a massage, and pretty close to as satisfying as a box of chocolates. (Well, kinda.) Even better, you can take an hour of "me time" for exercise every single day and nobody will judge you for being fancy or selfish. Instead, they will admire your dedication while you sweat yourself to a more peaceful and hotter you.

## Magical Benefit #7—It's Multitasking Heaven

Sometimes there's just too much shit that needs to get done for you to take an hour out for nothing but zoning out on the elliptical, but the cool thing about exercise is that you can do other things at the same time. You can ride your bike to work and get exercise during your commute, read your psychology text on the stationary bike, or check your BlackBerry from the treadmill. However, be careful not to multitask *too* much—if you're texting, reading a newspaper, and listening to a book on tape all while jogging up a steep trail, you are surely asking for trouble.

## Magical Benefit #8—You'll Get Sounder Sleep and Sweeter Dreams

No matter how tired you think you are, your body still needs exercise. In fact, one of the reasons you might be so tired is that you aren't exercising enough and getting that natural energy boost we already told you about. When you exercise consistently at the right intensity level, your body will naturally balance out your energy levels and sleep patterns. Adding exercise to your life will guarantee less tossing and turning at night, give you fewer nightmares, and make the idea of standing naked in front of a mirror less of a nightmare, too.

## Magical Benefit #9—You'll Power Through PMS

For one week of the month we completely hate our lives, and for two days of that week we are borderline homicidal. (Can you relate to this or are we crazy? Don't answer that.) Anyway, exercising during that time of the month not only improves your nasty-ass mood, but it will help out with water retention and painful cramps, too. Quit taking your pitiful PMS mood out on your husband, customers, kids, employees, and especially yourself, and instead work those hormonal issues out though your workout.

### Magical Benefit #10—It Boosts Confidence!

We saved the best (and most important) benefit for last. Making your body move and work in different ways really does help you feel like the Hot Chick that you are. It will remind you that your body is strong and capable, but also that you can't take it for granted. If you get winded after two minutes of walking slowly on a treadmill, we're pretty sure you're not feeling your best right now. But when you hike a giant mountain and then ride home on your bike, you will feel powerful and more confident than ever—we promise.

# Exercise Your Enjoyment!

Maybe you find exercise boring or hate going to the gym as much as we hate doing laundry, and if you're one of these girls, we feel sorry for you because you're missing out on all of the ways that exercise can be fun! What's that? Is that the sound of your pretty laughter? Well, you can laugh all the way to the gym with our tips for making exercise as enjoyable as a trip to the mall or a long soak in a tub. (Well, kinda.) Anyway, pull out that sports bra (the most supportive one you can find!), lace up those tennies, and get ready to finally enjoy your exercise!

### Exercise Enjoyment #1—Sweat and Socialize
Use your friends to make your workouts more fun and less painful. Go on a power walk together while bitching about your boss, take turns teaching each other a new sport, and then scream at each other (nicely) to do fifty push-ups. Instead of meeting your girls for brunch, meet at a yoga class or go for a hike together. You can even do a Pilates video together in your living room. If you don't have any friends then we're very sorry, but that's even more of a reason for you to go to the gym and make some.

### Exercise Enjoyment #2—Tune In and Tune Out
One of the best things about exercise is that it's one of the only times you can truly zone out while letting music power you through your workout. Plug in your MP3 player of choice and turn up whatever music gets your blood pumping. It will help you run faster, bike longer, and walk harder while making the time go by

in a flash. Pretty soon, you'll be looking forward to your workouts so that you can spend some quality time with your favorite bands.

### Exercise Enjoyment #3—Rags & Mags

Yes, we did talk a bunch of shit about tabloids in the last chapter, but we have no problem contradicting ourselves a little bit. That's part of what makes being a woman so much fun. Anyway, as long as you're sweating toxins out of your body while putting that toxic b.s. into your brain, we figure you'll come out about even. Our point is to get you to the gym, so if reading tabloids and beauty magazines helps motivate you, go for it. Of course, the gym is a great place to catch up on real journalism, too, so slip a copy of *Time* or *The New Yorker* in between your *Cosmo* and *Us Weekly* and your brain and booty will both be so much hotter.

### Exercise Enjoyment #4—Butt Class

Group fitness classes can be so much more fun than slogging away on the treadmill all alone. First of all, there's a hot teacher screaming at you to make sure you don't get lazy, they usually play fun music, and there's a group of people suffering right there with you. You work so much harder when there are people watching you, and our extremely unscientific studies show that you burn about twice the calories in an hour-long class as you do when left to your own devices.

### Exercise Enjoyment #5—Variety

Of course, if you do the same exercise every day, the minutes will pass slower than the microwave timer when you haven't eaten all day. Variety is not only the spice of life; it's the fun of life, too! Think about it—if you ate the same dinner every night, eventually you'd hate eating dinner, wouldn't you? And if you did the exact same thing in the bedroom every night . . . well, you get the idea. Make exercise part of your routine, but don't let it become too routine! Take a butt class♥ one day, jump on the elliptical the next, and try mat Pilates the day after. You'll stay motivated, feel energized, and working out will be more fun than you ever imagined.

# Fit in Fitness

How often do you hear someone say, "I'd love to work out but I don't have time," or, "I used to exercise but now I'm too busy"? Well, we are calling bullshit on people who say that, and we hope you're not one of them. You find time to maintain your Facebook page and watch *Mad Men*, so don't try to tell us you don't have time to exercise. You just aren't making time. What would you say if a guy with BMS♥ told you he couldn't date you because he's too busy with work? Well, we really hope you'd tell him that he's full of shit, and if he really wanted to see you he'd find a way to fit you in—you should do the same thing for exercise.

We know that some of you go to school full time, work full-time jobs, have three kids, are presidents of your co-op boards or home owners' associations, volunteer at hospitals, and belong to the PTA. We're very sorry that you are stressed to the max, but we think that's even more of a reason for you to make sure that you fit fitness into your life. You need to turn off your brain and let your body take the load for a while. Our bodies need exercise in order to thrive, and staying in shape can also help you stay sane by giving you more energy and a better mood with which to tackle all of your responsibilities.

You can do it. You can make fitness a priority and find a way to squeeze it in, whether it's by waking up super early to work out or scheduling conference calls around your favorite butt class♥ like we do. Unless you're allergic to your own sweat or paralyzed from the neck down (sorry, that's not funny), you have no excuse not to exercise. In fact, you're wasting a perfect, healthy body by abusing it with inactivity until it goes to shit. Just follow our five steps to fitting in fitness, put your lazy days behind you, and embrace your active heyday♥ without wasting another minute.

## Step 1—Acknowledge the Problem

Just like getting out of an abusive relationship, quitting smoking, or controlling an online shopping addiction, you can't change anything until you acknowledge the problem. If you're not exercising—and you know who you are—we are telling you right now that there's a problem. You can't deny it any longer. If you truly don't have time for exercise, you're going to have to cut something else out of your life. It's very simple. You are going to take responsibility for your health and your body right here and right now. Got it? Great! Now we can move on to fixing things.

## Step 2—Treat It as a Necessity

Joining a fancy gym that provides you with eucalyptus-scented towels and a fresh set of workout clothes every day may be a luxury, but exercise in and of itself is not. It truly is a necessity that is just as important to your body as sleep and food. Would you go weeks or months without food? Then you shouldn't go that long without activity, either. Without exercise, your muscles atrophy, your immune system weakens, and you *die sooner*. As soon as you start treating exercise as the necessity that it is, it will become a part of your life that you wouldn't dare skip—and that's how it should be.

## Step 3—Know You Deserve It

You may have many jobs in this life, but your most important job is to take care of yourself so that you are physically and mentally energized to do all of your other jobs! Do not feel guilty for one second about leaving your kids with a sitter to go to the gym or turning off your phone to take a spinning class during your lunch break. Your boss and kids will appreciate your clearheaded postworkout mind, and your man will love your post-workout body, so if you can't deal with doing something for you, just think of it as doing yet another thing for them.

## Step 4—Make a Plan

Sit down and go through every minute of your day until you find one hour each day to exercise. The time is there, we promise; you might just have to shift things around a little bit to find it. Do you meet a friend for lunch every Thursday? Meet her for a walk, instead. Do you watch two hours of TV each night? Do a workout video and then watch one hour, instead. Can you afford to drop off your laundry at a fluff and fold place and work out when you'd normally be doing laundry, instead? It doesn't matter when or how you do it; just mark out an hour of each day and set that plan in stone.

## Step 5—Follow Through

Don't get distracted, don't put it off for another day or another week, and don't even wait until you finish this book—listen to the good people at Nike and just do it! Don't break your pattern, but don't take an all-or-nothing approach, either. Take a day or a week off if you have strep throat or your Grandma dies, and then pick it right back up again without feeling guilty. If you fall off the exercise wagon, it's totally fine as long as you don't just lie there and let that wagon run you over. Simply get back on it and see how much your life changes from fitting fitness in!

# Body Basics

Exercise is one of those things that can involve numbers and math and make some girls want to tear out their eyelashes, so we're going to break down some basic exercise terms, nice and simple. If you were paying so little attention in health class that you don't know the difference between carbs and cardio, this section is for you. Pay attention now so that you can get your booty bouncing without any brain bewilderment.

**Cardio** is short for cardiovascular activity. The cardiovascular system includes the heart, blood, and blood vessels, so doing cardio exercise means that you are getting your heart pumping and your blood flowing. You don't need to measure your heart rate or anything boring like that, because you can tell whether or not you're doing cardio by how sweaty and breathless you are; you want to be actively sweating for over thirty minutes and be breathing harder than usual, but you *don't* want to be gasping desperately for air. Cardio is essential not only for losing weight, but also for strengthening your heart and lungs. Running, biking, swimming, climbing, kickboxing, jumping rope, power yoga, and hiking are all examples of cardio. If you're not half blind from sweat dripping in your eyes after these activities and your straightened hair has not gone curly, you are not really doing cardio.

*Note: You should do three to four hours of cardio per week, breaking it up into thirty- to fifty-minute sessions.*

**Cool Down** is a short period of low to moderate exercise at the end of your workout that brings your heart rate back to normal. If you run sprints for thirty minutes and then stop abruptly and jump in the shower, you'll get all dizzy when you try to shave your legs because your heart will still be beating too fast. You need to gently ease your heart back to reality with a five-minute cool down after any sort of workout to catch your breath and wipe off your sweat.

*Note: If you don't feel the need for a cool down, then you are wasting time and being lazy by not exercising hard enough.*

**High Impact Exercise** is technically an exercise where both feet leave the ground simultaneously, so any form of running or jumping is considered high impact exercise. The impact is great for strengthening your bones as well as burning calories, and it's usually the quickest way to get yourself all sweaty and breathless—but if you have bad knees, osteoporosis, or boobies that hurt when you bounce too much, low impact workouts might make more sense for your body.

*Note: Jumping jacks are a high impact exercise that you can do right in your living room!*

**Low Impact Exercise** is (duh) any form of exercise where you are *not* bouncing around like a cute little jumping bean. Yoga, Pilates, and swimming are all great examples of low impact exercises. Low impact exercise is much gentler on the body because there is no pounding on the joints and no bouncing boobies, but it still burns calories and gets your heart rate up if you stick with it.

*Note: Be kind to your body by alternating between high and low impact exercise. Take a yoga class one day and an '80s-style step class the next.*

**Resistance Training** is the same thing as strength training, which is anything that uses resistance to force your hot muscles to contract. You can do resistance training by doing biceps curls with hand weights, working on any machine that resembles a Bowflex, or doing lunges and squats in butt class♥ while using weighted balls (he, he). Push-ups, pull-ups, and yoga are also ways of doing resistance training because you are working against your own body weight!

*Note: You should do at least two hours of resistance training a week and break it up into two to four sessions. Remember to do at least ten or twenty minutes of cardio first to warm up your muscles.*

**Stretching** elongates your muscles, which in turn increases flexibility. Being flexible is not just a job requirement for strippers; every Hot Chick should be flexible for more than the obvious reasons. Flexibility can save your life if your building collapses in an earthquake and you have to stay balled up in a space the size of a microwave until somebody finds you, makes it easier for you to walk in four-inch heels without twisting your ankle, and keeps your muscles feeling less tense. No matter how hot your body looks, if you can't touch your toes, you've got problems. You must stretch for at least five full minutes after every workout.

*Note: Take a yoga class to learn some cool new stretches and then use these poses to spice up your love life!*

**Target Heart Rate** is the number of pumps you want your heart to make per minute during your workout. Now, a target heart rate varies from Hot Chick to Hot Chick depending on your age, weight, and general fitness level, so use those cheesy posters at the gym to figure out your exact number for yourself. But please don't get too hung up on exact numbers here; it's most important that you work out in a zone where you're sweating, a little breathless, but still able to hold up your end of a conversation (hopefully not with the smelly dude next to you).

*Note: Your goal should be to stay in your target heart rate zone for the majority of your workout and include little bursts of cardio that take you just above that zone. Then use your cool down to bring your heart rate back to normal.*

# Fabulous Favorites

Because we are so freaking nice, we'd never spend all this time making sure you work out and teaching you all the terminology without sharing some of our favorite *ways* to work out with all you Hot Chicks. Workout regimes are just like relationships; if they're boring, uninspiring, and passionless, you'll want to cheat on them (and Hot Chicks don't cheat)—but if you take tips from your girlfriends and keep things exciting, you'll stay faithful forever! So have fun trying out our top ten list and then make one of your own.

## Fabulous Favorite #1—Spinning

Other than the fact that we're worried that those tiny bike seats will prevent us from ever having children, spinning classes are a great workout. The instructors usually turn off the lights, put on good music, and help you leave this zero impact, intense cardio session a super sweaty Hot Chick. You get almost all of the benefits of running but without your boobies bouncing all over the place, so it's a win-win! Don't be afraid to turn up the resistance; it will make for a better workout and will keep you from spinning out of control and flying into the sweaty guy on the next bike.

*Trusty Tip: Unless you have a really bony butt that bruises easily, you don't have to wear those ugly padded cycling shorts that look like a grown-up diaper, and you don't have to waste money on those funky spinning shoes, either. Regular workout clothes will work just fine.*

## Fabulous Favorite #2—Power Walking

We used to run, but after so many years dealing with knee issues, shin splints, and the lack of truly supportive sports bras in this world (does anyone have a tip for that they can share with us?), we gave it up. The good news is that the treadmill can still be your best friend if you put it at a 15 percent incline and walk at least three miles per hour. If you switch back and forth between walking faster at a lower incline and slower at a high incline, your ass will love you—and pretty soon you'll love it back.

*Trusty Tip:* **Listen to music and switch up the speed and incline when the songs change! You'll be your own personal, personal trainer and the time will go by quicker.**

### Fabulous Favorite #3—Power Yoga
You might suck at first, but don't be intimidated or give up. Eventually you will able to contort yourself into a pretzel and stand on your head while just barely breaking a pretty, glistening sweat. Yoga works every muscle in the body, from your abs and butt to muscles you never knew you had—but it also calms your mind, and many people believe that it keeps you looking young. We're not sure if that's true, but it's better for you than Botox, and we're going to try it until we're positive it's not working.

*Trusty Tip:* **There's a lot of major exhaling in yoga, so don't eat a giant heap of garlic laden pasta just beforehand or everyone in class will hate you.**

### Fabulous Favorite #4—Pilates
There are two types of Pilates: the kind where you use resistance to tone your muscles on a machine called a reformer and the kind you do on a mat that is something like the baby of a yoga class and a *Buns of Steel* video from the '80s. Your gym might not offer either form of Pilates and you may not even know how to pronounce it

correctly, but we still encourage you to seek it out. Pilates is great low impact exercise, and it's the only workout that you can do (in public) while lying flat on your back.

*Trusty Tip: Joseph Pilates originally invented Pilates for boxers in the early 1900s, and it has since been used by professional dancers, Madonna, Jennifer Anniston, and Jennifer Garner. We're not saying you should try to live your life like a celebrity, but these people have some of the best bodies on earth, so this Pilates stuff is certainly worth a try!*

## Fabulous Favorite #5—Kickboxing

These classes can be so painful that you just want to die, but as soon as it's over you get a euphoric, Zen-like feeling and magically♥ forget how much it sucked. It's kind of like how women go through childbirth and then have more babies because of the hormone rush that blisses them out just after giving birth. We think if they remembered the pain clearly they'd never have unprotected sex again. Kickboxing can be just as rewarding as childbirth, but without all the spit up and lack of sleep.

*Trusty Tip: Not only do kickboxing classes make you feel strong and powerful, but they let you get out so much aggression and negative energy through kicking and punching. Bonus!*

## Fabulous Favorite #6—Free Weights

You can either grab some hand weights and find a corner to work out in or brave the free weight area where tons of dudes are grunting, and spotting each other, and doing all kinds of other hot stuff like that. In either case, use five- to ten-pound weights to do biceps curls, triceps kickbacks, lunges, squats, and dead lifts. If you don't know what we're talking about, take a butt class♥ and then mimic those same moves on your own. Remember that building muscle helps burn fat by increasing your metabolism, meaning that you'll burn extra calories even when you're snuggled up on the couch watching *Lost*.

*Trusty Tip: Always wear sneakers when lifting weights, even if you're doing it at home. If you drop a weight on your bare foot, the nail will turn black, fall off, and be fucked up♥ for like a year. (Not that we know from experience or anything.)*

### Fabulous Favorite #7—The Elliptical
This is another great machine for getting a low impact cardio workout. It's less agonizing than running and more of a full body workout than the bike—the best of both worlds. Be warned that you may feel a little bit wonky at first if you're not super coordinated, but once you get used to it, you can play with the speed and incline just like on a treadmill. Hop on one of these bad boys for forty minutes and soon your body will be getting a lot of attention from some other bad boys.

*Trusty Tip: If you do it right, you will be literally dripping with sweat after five minutes, so make sure you wipe the elliptical machine down with a towel when you're done. There is nothing grosser than using a piece of equipment that looks like it was left outside during a monsoon.*

### Fabulous Favorite #8—Hiking
Hiking is one of the best outdoor exercises because you can challenge yourself on those inclines while communing with nature and soaking up some Vitamin D—but if you live someplace that's

as flat as Kate Hudson, that's no excuse for you not to move it in the sunshine. Take a fast walk around your neighborhood or ride your bike to school. This is a great way to commit yourself to a full hour of exercise because if you go thirty minutes away by bike or foot, you've got to get yourself back (and don't you dare call a cab)!

*Trusty Tip: Remember to be safe and protect both your skin and your hide. That means wear sunscreen, stay alert for cars and psychos, and always tell someone where you're going.*

## Fabulous Favorite #9—Swimming

If you have knee or joint problems that are so bad that even the bike or the elliptical are too high impact, swimming is probably your answer. They make it look so easy in the Olympics, but this is really a badass workout that will give you a fantastic ass. Try swimming laps and don't be ashamed to take a class if you never learned to swim properly. You can also try water aerobics classes, but stay away if you have a problem with seeing a ninety-year-old woman in a swimsuit.

*Trusty Tip: Don't forget your goggles and if you have really bad eyesight, you might have to invest in a prescription pair. We've seen what happens when you wear regular glasses in a chlorinated pool, and it's not pretty.*

## Fabulous Favorite #10—Butt Class

Once again, we saved the best for last! This is literally our favorite form of exercise on the planet for so many reasons. It tones your entire body in a fun group environment, but the best part about it is that there's someone else there doing all of the thinking for you. All you have to do is follow his or her instructions while indulging in all sorts of fantasy sequences♥ and you'll get a brain break while simultaneously getting a better body!

*Trusty Tip: Don't you dare feel LSE♥ or compare yourself to the other women in these classes, and don't worry that they're looking at you and your so-called flaws. Remember that all of those women are just as LSE♥ as you and are probably only worried about themselves.*

# The Truth about Exercise

When you order an ab-roller that promises a six pack after just five minutes a day, they neglect to inform you that no matter how much you roll it, your stomach won't shrink an inch if you fill it with Oreos. Losing weight and staying in shape is about burning more calories than you consume, so eating right is completely connected to exercise. If you reward yourself for thirty minutes at the gym with five hundred calories of chocolate, you'll actually *gain* weight, and spending hours of your life exercising just to go straight to the KFC drive-through is like wasting a year of your life and forty thousand dollars planning a wedding just to kill your husband on your honeymoon like those crazy people on *Dateline*. It's a waste of time and energy, not to mention completely self-destructive and self-defeating.

We've totally been there, and we know how frustrating it is to spend hours at the gym and then accidentally sabotage yourself by drinking an entire bottle of champagne, eating the tops off of twelve cupcakes, and then drunkenly consuming a punch-sized bowl of guacamole. We know that doing this can make you feel LSE♥, guilty, ashamed, and like you never want to set foot in a gym ever again for the rest of your life. On the other hand, when you eat those three squares a day and treat yourself to a glass of wine and a cookie or two at night, you'll feel confident, empowered, and ready to kick the shit out of your next workout. This book (and the whole concept of living like a Hot Chick) is all about finding balance, and finding the right balance between eating right, occasional indulgences, and exercise is essential for you to feel like the Hot Chick that you are.

As you make a plan to start a workout routine, it's important to take this opportunity to think about what you're feeding those pretty muscles of yours. Are you eating too much? Are you not eating enough? Is your diet full of sugar, chemicals, and fat instead or fruits, vegetables, and protein? We're going to help you through the details in the next chapter, but for now we want you to remember that your food and exercise routines have to complement and support each other, not impair or disrupt each other. When you feel good about everything you put into your body and confident in the way you move and work your body, you will be feeling and living like a true Hot Chick.

# Chapter 3

## *Eat It Up*

AS YOU ALREADY KNOW, OUR GOAL IN ALL OF OUR BOOKS IS TO GUIDE ALL OF YOU HOT CHICKS THROUGH EVERY PHASE OF YOUR LIVES. We started with *How to Eat Like a Hot Chick* because so much of women's self-esteem centers around food. If we can't enjoy a bowl of pasta, it's virtually impossible for us to feel confident in our bodies, relationships, jobs, and places in this world. However, once we learn how to properly feed our bodies and indulge without guilt, it is so much easier to feel strong and confident in every aspect of our lives. We helped each other reach this point and we wrote that first book to help you get there, too.

But if you think we've already said everything we have to say on the subject of women and food, you are dead wrong. There are three reasons we're writing another chapter about it. First, our publisher told us to, so we didn't really have much of a choice. Second, we started speaking to many of you after the publication of *How to Eat Like a Hot Chick* and realized that for the most part, women are even more fucked up♥ about food than we thought. You need more help, and we want to give it to you! Finally, we are a few years older and wiser than we were when we wrote that first book, and over the past few years, our own relationships with food have changed. We can finally live with a jar of peanut butter in the house without eating the whole thing at once, we don't eat frozen yogurt for lunch anymore, and, truth be told, we've been going through bottles of olive oil almost as quickly as Rachael Ray. Now we're excited to share our new ideas about food with all of you.

You can't live like a Hot Chick or feel like one if you are not eating like one. Remember that if a Hot Chick is a confident woman, eating like one means eating with confidence, and that is what we're talking about here. Our goal in this chapter is to get you to look at food differently—as something that fuels your entire life, and is also a fun source of pleasure, not a torture device or something to avoid. We want you to feed your body well, nourish it, and splurge with confidence and passion so that food makes you energized and happy instead of remorseful and lethargic. It's time to stop the self-torment and obsession and truly start enjoying food, celebrating it, and finding a balance that will ultimately set you free.

# An Obsession with Torture

Women don't just torture themselves about food; they seem to love nothing more than brutalizing each other, too. We can't seem to ask for half-and-half in a restaurant without the waitress making a nasty comment about milk fat or eat a plate of pasta without a woman at the next table commenting on our consumption of empty carbs. This is just another way that women make life harder for each other, by spreading their issues with food faster than the swine flu. We women are complicit in this, but so is the diet industry. That entire industry is on a mission to instill fear in all of us about regular food, and by the looks of things, they're doing a pretty good job of it. They want us to be so afraid of pizza, dessert, and lemonade that we'll pay them infinite amounts of money to tell us that we can eat these foods as long as they have their company's name on the packaging. They want us to believe that if we don't eat their food, count their points, or supplement with their particular brand of bullshit, we will never be sexy or desirable. They want us to live in such fear of regular eating habits that they can turn around and sell us on their completely unrealistic claims. When you think about it, of course the same woman who's so brainwashed by Atkins that she's terrified of a banana is going to believe that she can eat huge amounts of pre-packaged chocolate cake and hamburgers and lose a hundred pounds overnight. This woman has been so confused into submission that she's (literally) eating out of the diet industry's greedy little hand.

Humans weren't made to control their food like this. Tell a woman that she's starting a diet on Monday, and the first thing she'll do is eat an entire gallon of peanut butter cup ice cream. Can you blame her? This poor woman lives in a world where her peers don't allow her to enjoy her food, the tabloids tell her that she's fat, and a thousand companies insist that she can lose inordinate amounts of weight instantly if she forks over her hard-earned paycheck. These are all lies. Sure, you might lose ten pounds by eating a shake for breakfast, another for lunch, and a teeny, tiny dinner, or by eating cereal for three meals a day, but as soon as you go back to eating real food, you'll gain those ten pounds back along with another twenty because you'll have no idea how to balance your diet. In this case, the diet industry is succeeding by making you live in such fear and confusion that you'll go crawling back to them on your hands and knees with your credit card out, begging for another shake or another bowl of cereal.

This is a horrible environment for any women to live in, and too many of us are living in fear of the very thing that is supposed to give us energy, power, nutrition, and enjoyment. By obsessing over food, we are wasting too much time, missing out on so much fun, and passing this negative thought pattern onto our baby girls, who are born into this world perfect and hungry. It's time to find some balance, to start feeding our bodies well, and to begin treating ourselves to pleasure.

# Stop the Insanity

You know that fad diets will never help you get healthy or reach your weight goals and that the diet industry is just a giant conspiracy to make billions of dollars by keeping us confused and afraid; you're ready to find balance when it comes to food. Put all of that negativity behind you, and let us help you stop the insanity.

**Step 1—Know That You Are a Hot Chick**
In order to have a healthy relationship with food you must know that you are hot enough, powerful enough, smart enough, and together enough to have a healthy relationship with food. It's just like your love life—if you don't believe that you deserve a great boyfriend, you will never find a great boyfriend. We already know that you're a Hot Chick who deserves to feel good about yourself, but it's time for you to embrace that inner Hot Chick and start acting (and eating) like her.

**Step 2—If You Want It, Eat It**
The best way to combat food issues is to look them in the face and say, "Fuck you, food issues!" If you're craving something, stop wasting hours of your life trying not to eat it and just eat it. Eat it every single day and your obsession with it will fade like our tan lines after what seems like five minutes. We love sweets, particularly chocolate, and so we eat chocolate every single day of our lives. Yes, we're serious. We're not talking about an entire king-sized bag of peanut M&M's, but we do eat a piece of chocolate or a cookie or something every night instead of tormenting ourselves until we give in and eat the whole bag.

### Step 3—Stock Your House

You know what else we do with chocolate? We fill our houses with it! We have so much freaking chocolate in our houses that Willie Wonka would be jealous. Another great way to stop obsessing about food is to make a statement to yourself and the universe♥ that you can have chocolate and chips and whatever else tempts you in your face 24/7 and still have self-control. Remember that acting confident can actually make you feel confident, just like how acting heydayish♥ can actually make you feel heydayish♥. Keeping gallons of ice cream in your kitchen is a pretty bold move when you love ice cream just as much as you love your dog, but acting confident enough to have a freezer full of Dove bars can actually make you secure enough to not eat the whole box in one sitting.

### Step 4—If You Fall Off the Wagon, Get Back On

So what happens if you do fuck up♥ and eat that whole box of Dove bars in one sitting? Do you cry and beat your chest as you work your way through everything else in your freezer, including the things that you don't recognize, or do you say, "Oops, I fucked up♥, but I'll get back in balance tomorrow"? Remember that having a good relationship with food is a lifelong process and not an overnight transformation, so there are going to be bumps in the road. Again, let's compare it to your love life—if you love a guy enough to marry him, would you file for divorce after one bad fight or would you stick it out, make up, and let the love carry you through? Well, then you should love yourself enough not to give up so easily on yourself, either.

### Step 5—Stop Spending, Start Cooking

You can nurture your relationship with food by working with it, being creative with it, and then enjoying what you've created!

We don't care how un-domestic you think you are; search online for some fun recipes or watch a few hours of the Food Network and get excited about picking out gorgeous produce and cooking yourself some healthy and delicious meals. Make sure dessert is on the menu, too, and enjoy the process without fear of inhaling it all before it's even in the oven. This will help you appreciate and honor food in a whole new way. No excuses, ladies! If you can read, count, and press buttons, you can totally cook—so get started now.

# The Beauty of Balance

Striking the right balance is essential to happiness and success in every part of your life, from business to relationships to food. We live in an all-or-nothing society; many women go from eating Big Macs every night to swearing off high fructose corn syrup for eternity, but they will never cease to be tormented by food until they balance out their diets. Now, when we say, "balanced diet," we are not referring to that silly food pyramid thing that tells you to eat *eleven* servings of bread a day. (Who do they think they're kidding?) We are talking about finding a balance between healthy, nourishing foods and fun, delicious indulgences. That means cooking most of your meals with foods from the earth that are full of vitamins and nutrients—and then leaving yourself room every now and then to enjoy fucked up ♥ chocolate chip pancakes that are covered in whipped cream *and* syrup or a giant plate of fried chicken and doughy biscuits drizzled in warm honey butter. (Our mouths are totally watering right now.)

Balance can mean taking a cookie break in the middle of a long workday or eating chocolate cake for breakfast and a pound of spinach for dinner (our favorite). It's about living somewhere comfortable and easy in between the two extremes. Obviously, exercise and a balanced diet go together like peanut butter and chocolate (or pepperoni and pizza, if you're more of a savory-craving Hot Chick) because working out helps make room for all those indulgences. Remember, we're not saying that you need to punish yourself with an hour on the treadmill if you eat a wheel of brie and a pint of Ben & Jerry's. We're just reminding you that an hour of cardio will help you feel like the Hot Chick that you are after that kind of a dairy fest. It's a fine line, but an important one, because Hot Chicks eat right and exercise in order to feel even better about themselves, not to chastise themselves for slipping up.

Everyone wants a magic ♥ pill or potion that will make her look and feel perfectly hot, and we're here to tell you that we found it. Seriously, we have the secret solution to feeling sexy, and it's not an herb or lotion or nasty-ass, sugar-free protein water. Nope. It's balance—and we're going to show you how to find that balance so that you can love your body and your life, too. We're going to describe our system in mathematical terms because the cool thing about math is that it is always logical, with no room for excuses or gray areas. Two pairs of shoes will always equal four separate shoes, a five-hundred-dollar paycheck minus seven hundred dollars' worth of shoes will always leave you in debt, and the same concept can be applied to food, exercise, and combining the two in order to balance out your life. Don't you dare be intimidated or tell us that you hate math! Just read these equations and let them inspire you to find the beauty of balance in your own life.

# Hot Chick Algebra

**1.** Three slices of pizza + a giant bowl of ice cream + nineteen handfuls of popcorn on the couch with your man on Sunday night = a cup of black coffee + a bowl of oatmeal + two giant salads + a forty-five-minute run on Monday.

**2.** An apple with almond butter for breakfast + a spinach salad for lunch + 1 spin class = two glasses of champagne + a hunk of brie cheese + five buttery crackers + four fried appetizers at your best friend's engagement party.

**3.** Three rum & Cokes + two beers + the Taco Bell drive-through at 3:00 a.m. = a gallon of water and a giant spinach salad for breakfast when you wake up at noon with indigestion and a headache.

**4.** Eating your roommate's entire jar of peanut butter at midnight = two liters of water + a bowl of watermelon for breakfast + the cost of buying her a brand new jar before she wakes up.

**5.** Two poached eggs with flourless whole grain bread for breakfast + replacing mayo with a schmear of goat cheese on your veggie sandwich at lunch = A yummy pink cupcake at your coworker's birthday party that afternoon.

**6.** Drinking a bottle of water instead of a glass of juice for breakfast + drinking a bottle of water instead of a soda at lunch = two sour apple martinis at happy hour that night.

**7.** One week of yoga after work each day + avoiding white flour and sugar = chocolate cake for breakfast while you watch *The Bachelor* on your TiVo.

**8.** A PMS binge of four doughnuts + one entire sleeve of Girl Scout cookies + chicken fingers dipped in ranch dressing = one butt class♥ + six glasses of water + two Midol + a giant spinach salad for dinner.

**9.** Greasy Chinese takeout + four glasses of boxed wine + a fight with your boyfriend + all of the leftover apple pie at 11:00 p.m. = an early morning run to clear your head and heart, sweat out the toxins, and burn off some calories.

**10.** No breakfast + five Twizzlers at your desk + fast food for lunch + one frozen dinner = you not feeling like a Hot Chick.

# Finding Food Balance
## at Work and at Play

Food at work can be an obstacle, a fun distraction, a bonding tool, or a monkey on your back—depending on how you handle it. Many of you who are stuck in an office all day start planning what you're going to eat for lunch the minute you log onto your email in the morning, and others of you go full steam ahead and don't eat a thing until happy hour, but neither of these options is very balanced or healthy.

When playtime comes around, it's hard to know the difference between a healthy indulgence and an obnoxious pig-out session, or how to celebrate with food without going further overboard than Goldie Hawn. Since this book is about finding balance between work and play, we want you to feel as confident and satisfied with the food you eat on the job as you do about the stuff you consume after hours. Our dos and don'ts to eating like a Hot Chick at work and play will help you with exactly that.

**At Work:**

**Do #1—Eat Breakfast**
We do not mean that you should go to Denny's and eat a Grand Slam before work every day, but eating a bowl of oatmeal, a slice of whole grain toast with peanut butter, or some fruit and a hard-boiled egg will get your metabolism pumping, energize and sharpen your hot brain, and ensure that you won't die of LBS♥ when your eleven o'clock meeting runs long. Lord knows that if you scarf down a chocolate-filled croissant between subway stops you'll barely even taste it, so save the fried French toast and other deca-

dent stuff for special occasions and stick to something small and healthy for every day.

### Do #2—Break for Snacks

Your eyes need a break from that computer screen, your limbs need to stand up and stretch, and the rest of your body needs some fuel to keep you going all day long. Your snack shouldn't have much more than two hundred calories, but it should be tasty and give you something to look forward to when the hours are ticking by at a deathly slow rate. Remember to keep it balanced! That means if you ate a piece of ziti pizza for lunch you should snack on something like an apple and twelve almonds, but if you ate a salad for lunch and then your boss announced impending layoffs, feel free to eat something more indulgent like two cookies, three fun-sized Snickers, or a small bag of chips.

### Do #3—Do Lunch

You wouldn't drive for eight hours without filling up your tank, so don't you dare do that to your body! Remember that you are a Hot Chick who feeds her body nutritious food from the earth, so don't spend your lunch hour waiting in line to microwave your bullshit frozen meal or going through a drive-through. The turkey, avocado, and veggie sandwich you make at home will be so much healthier (and even cheaper) than a five-dollar foot-long from Subway, and the leftover pasta with veggies that you cook will feel gourmet compared to an unidentifiable frozen food block from Lean Cuisine. Remember to make lunch fun and plan weekly lunches with your coworkers or friends. Seeing a friendly face in the middle of your workday can do wonders for the rest of your afternoon.

## Do #4—Remember There's No Such Thing as a Free Lunch

If you're one of those Hot Chicks with a corporate job that involves daily business lunches, you've probably already noticed what it's doing to your waistline and your self-esteem. So many of us get so excited by the idea of an expensed lunch that we end up ordering three courses at noon, or else we feel pressured by our dining companions to join them in doing so. Of course we want you to enjoy these meals, but if you want to feel like a Hot Chick you have to remember to keep it balanced. So if you eat lunch at a steakhouse, perhaps you should even it out by tossing a giant salad for dinner, or if you have plans to go out for Mexican for dinner, skip the appetizer and dessert and just order a light entrée at lunch. If your coworkers make some nasty backhanded comments about your eating habits, which they inevitably will, just act like the Hot Chick you are and say something like, "I feel better when I eat this way; how's that daily porterhouse working for you?"

## Do #5—Plan For Dinner

There is nothing worse than getting home from a long, hard day with simultaneous giant cases of OWL♥ and LBS♥ to find no food in the house and no clue as to what you should eat for dinner. This can only lead you one place—the take-out menu drawer—and we don't want to find you there every night. Planning ahead even by just a few hours will save you time and money because you can load up on groceries during your lunch break or check in with your man and see if he can take care of dinner that night. Of course, thinking further ahead and cooking a bunch of meals on Sunday works even better, but we know that might be too much to ask.

## Don't #1—Eat Mindlessly

Don't thoughtlessly grab one of the tasteless cookies your coworker brings in every day or fill your plate with nasty, processed mini-muffins at your morning meetings. It may have been a good reason to hike Everest, but Hot Chicks don't eat things just because they're there. Foods with no nutritional value should be eaten as fun splurges, so only eat them if they are indeed enjoyable. Go to the bakery down the road with a colleague and indulge in a homemade muffin break or hold your next meeting over cappuccinos at a local coffee house instead of in your grubby cubicle, but stop mindlessly chewing on Starbursts in between emails and dropping cookie crumbs into your already germ-infested keyboard. Make your indulgences truly special and you'll enjoy them a whole lot more.

## Don't #2—Drink Mindlessly

Stop drinking half a dozen ice-blended coffee things, bubble teas, and other sugary nonsense throughout the day and switch to water right now. We know that some of you are drinking this shit just to occupy your mind and give your mouth something fun to do (and this is way better than blowing your boss, so good job) but you're still fucking up♥ because the calories in these beverages really add up. An ice-blended coffee in the morning followed by a sweetened iced tea with lunch and two sodas in the afternoon comes to almost a thousand calories. That is more than half of the calories you should be consuming in an entire day. Don't think you're being smart by drinking a case of Diet Cokes a day, either. It may have zero calories, but that shit is full of cancer-causing chemicals that make you puffy and mess with your blood sugar. If you need bubbly flavored drinks to get you through your day, try drinking flavored seltzer or mineral water instead and see how much hotter you feel!

## Don't #3—Eat at Your Desk

First of all, your desk is a total germ factory, and eating off it is literally worse than eating off of a toilet seat or sharing mascara with that assistant who keeps getting pinkeye. Second, multitasking while you eat isn't a good idea. You end up eating more than you normally would because you don't feel satisfied, and of course you don't feel satisfied when you're thoughtlessly shoveling in forkfuls of salad while typing out emails and using a pencil to dig crouton crumbs out of your keyboard. Does that sound like the way a Hot Chick would eat? Take a break, whether it's for five minutes or fifty, and go sit anywhere else while you eat. Your mind, your stomach, the janitor, and probably even your boss will all thank you.

**Don't #4—Bitch About Food**
Food is always present in the workplace and you need to handle it like the Hot Chick that you are. If we hear that you say, "I'm so upset that these brownies are good because now I'm tempted to eat them," we are going to come to your office and punch you in the face. Brownies are *supposed* to be good; why the hell would you wish they weren't? Change the way you think and talk about food at work. That means saying, "Hey, Betsy, thanks for bringing in these cookies," instead of, "Betsy, you are evil; why are you torturing us with all these cookies?!" Help us spread this Hot Chick attitude about food and hopefully soon we'll all be able to stop obsessing about this crap and get back to work.

**Don't #5—Be the Food Police**
You should never make a comment about what another Hot Chick (or guy) is or isn't eating, but this is especially true at work. You have no idea what is going on with other people—why your cubicle mate subsists on exclusively golden raisins or the girl down the hall eats the garnish off of the family-sized spare rib platter—and gossiping or commenting (even if you mean well) will only make you look nasty and LSE♥. You also never know when you'll hit a sensitive spot with your boss or the CEO, so shut up, do your

job, and focus on making your own eating habits as good as they can be.

**At Play:**

**Do #1—Eat Real Food on a Date**
Why on earth would you pretend not to be hungry, pick at your food, or order a side salad for dinner just to impress a guy? You should order that juicy steak or plate of French fries or whatever the hell you're in the mood for and enjoy eating it as much as the guy is enjoying being out on a date with someone as hot as you! If you skip dinner on the date we know you're going to go home starving and end up eating your whole house, so you might as well save yourself the calories, guilt, and indigestion and eat a real meal, instead.

**Do #2—Eat What Mother Earth Made For You**
Before we totally kill our planet, take the opportunity to load up on the food that grows out of the ground, in a tree, or on a vine. Hot Chicks need fruits and vegetables just like babies need their mothers' milk. The vitamins, minerals, and antioxidants from fruit and veggies will keep you looking and feeling hot, so use some creativity to make them fun. Puree some mangos, add some tequila and ice, and blend that goodness up into a healthy margarita, bake a fresh peach pie for that barbecue instead of making lame brownies that come from (and taste like) a cardboard box, and throw bananas and blueberries into the batter when you make pancakes for the cute boy you just had a magic♥ night with.

**Do #3—Celebrate with Food Every Month**
Instead of worrying about going off your diet, make a plan to celebrate with a coconut-covered chocolate bunny cake on Easter and a margarita and guacamole fest on Cinco de Mayo. It may sound

counterintuitive, but this will actually make it easier to eat well on "regular" days. Circle the holidays on your calendar and know that by enjoying these celebrations you are striking a healthy balance and healing your food issues by making food fun.

### Do #4—Pick Your Poison

What happens when you mix tequila, red wine, vodka tonics, and mudslides? You turn into a puffy, nauseous, and quite possibly slutty mess. The same thing can happen with food, so pick your poison when indulging and stick with it. Yes, we want you to go out and celebrate with food every chance you get, but don't forget that a calorie is still a calorie, and if you consume too many of them you won't end up feeling your best. If you're eating a cheesy, greasy pizza for dinner, then skip the cheesy, greasy appetizers, and if you want a sugary piña colada after dinner, think about passing on the lemon meringue pie—or just quit spreading sticks of butter on your bread and save those fatty calories for a bowl of lobster bisque or a slice of flourless chocolate cake. Pick your poison and you'll be able to enjoy every sinful bite.

### Do #5—Eat Magical♥ Foods

You already know that you should eat whole foods from the earth, but don't forget about the magical♥ benefits of green tea, plain Greek yogurts, and (dare we say it?) . . . olive oil! Also, herbs and spices are just as good for your body as apples and spinach, so don't be shy about adding cayenne pepper, cinnamon, basil, or cilantro when cooking up a celebratory feast. Your food will taste so much better, and these special foods do really cool things like boost your metabolism, help you digest fats, and possibly help cancel out the toxins from all of those martinis!

**Don't #1—Starve Yourself for Weeks Just to Pig Out at a Party**

So many women starve themselves for ages to look and feel hot in their little black dresses at a wedding or reunion, and then once the trays of appetizers start being passed, they go completely apeshit and eat everything as fast as they can. This is yet another way that food is just like sex—it shouldn't be used as a punishment or a reward. Depriving yourself just sets you up for an out of control binge. Instead, work out and eat well so that you can show up at that party feeling like the Hot Chick that you are and have a blast sampling mini meatballs and cheesecake bites without turning into some sort of crazed, crumb-covered cookie monster.

**Don't #2—Ever Turn Down Birthday Cake**

We're not trying to threaten you or anything, but we are a little bit superstitious, and we think that turning down a piece of someone's birthday cake (especially your own!) is like toasting with water—meaning that it's definitely rude and probably bad luck. Have your cake and please, please, *please* eat it, too!

**Don't #3—Eat Fast Food**

Fast food is not real food, so if you wouldn't dream of eating your patent leather high heels for lunch or snacking on lip gloss when you get hungry before dinner, we don't think there is any reason to eat chemical laden crap from a drive-through restaurant, either. When a taco costs as much as a gum ball or a burger is the same price as a wet n wild nail polish, we think there's something really fishy going on. The one exception to this very important rule is when you're drunk off your ass at 3:00 a.m. We think that maybe soaking up the alcohol toxins with a bunch of other toxins

can help cancel the first toxins out. We haven't quite proven this
theory yet, but it makes perfect sense to us.

### Don't #4—Be Afraid To Be a Food Snob

We love to eat "bad" food, but you will never catch us eating food
that's actually *bad*. It's just not worth it. After getting food poisoning one too many times from chain restaurants, we decided that
life is too short to eat things that might actually make our lives
even shorter. We give you full permission to refuse foods that look
gross, manmade, packaged, or full of chemicals. Go ahead and
be picky; spend your calories on things that actually taste good!
Instead of a box of Twinkies, eat a fresh, warm, cream-filled pas-
try from a real bakery. Decide that you are too cool for Pizza Hut
(which is totally fast food, by the way—stop kidding yourself) and
bake your own pizza at home with fresh dough that's only a $1.99
at Trader Joe's! Be a snob when it comes to food and your "bad"
attitude will make you feel better.

### Don't #5—Let Food Issues Snowball

The next time you're hanging out with your girlfriends and one
of them says, "I can't believe I ate that cookie; I'm such a fatty,"
don't reply by saying, "Well, I ate an entire Philly cheese steak, so
I'm even fatter." This will only lead to a giant bitch session like
that scene in *Mean Girls* where they resort to complaining about
their ankles. Don't take your friend's bait by saying, "No, you're so
skinny," either. This will just fuel her LSE♥ and constant need for
validation. Set a good example by changing the subject entirely
and all of your friends will be better off for it.

# Part II

## How to Work Like a Hot Chick

IT'S POSSIBLE THAT YOU MAY BE ONE LUCKY HOT CHICK WITH A TRUST FUND, A HUSBAND WHO MAKES SIX FIGURES, OR A ROYAL TITLE (OR EVEN BETTER, ALL THREE). If that's the case, then hooray for you! You can skip this part of the book. But millions of us struggle tirelessly trying to balance our work and personal lives. More often than not, work wins hands down, and many of us are working our hot little booties so hard that we are totally dying inside. To make matters worse, many of the same women who spend the majority of their time and energy at work aren't even working like Hot Chicks (by our definition) because they're so overwhelmed, stressed out, and unsure about how to work it at work. Does being assertive in the workplace means being a bitch or being a ball buster—and how are we supposed to manage to at once act feminine and aggressive, strong and womanly? Is this even possible?

Well, we are here to remind you that you deserve to have a work life that is as rewarding and fulfilling as it is challenging, and we are going to hold your pretty hand and guide you through the increasingly competitive career jungle as we show you how easy it can be to act like a confident, empowered Hot Chick in the workplace. Once you start truly working like a Hot Chick and using all of your inner power and goodness to get ahead in your career, the rest of your life will start to feel more balanced and magical♥, too!

# Chapter 4

## *Business Basics*

WHILE THE ECONOMY STAYS IN THE SHITTER AND HOT CHICKS ARE GETTING LAID OFF RIGHT AND LEFT, THERE ISN'T ANY ROOM FOR THE REST OF US TO FUCK UP♥ AT WORK. Almost every day we feel like we're going to die from the pressure to stay motivated, cheerful, and productive enough to make ends meet, and we know we're not alone. So what's the solution? How do we stay optimistic during this difficult time? Well, we think it's for all women to start working like Hot Chicks during every slowly passing moment of every endless workday.

There are basic, seemingly harmless things you might be doing every day that are actually preventing you from working like a Hot Chick. Maybe it's playing small♥, going in every morning with a foonge face♥, or acting lazy, unproductive, and unprofessional. Let's compare work to our favorite thing—your love life. If you wore a ketchup-stained shirt on a date and the next morning accidentally sent a thank you email to the wrong guy, you'd probably never hear from him again; if you act this sloppy and scatter-brained at work, you're probably not feeling the love there, either.

Changing simple behaviors can have a huge impact on the rest of your life, from helping you make more money to discovering your true calling (or, at the very least, preventing everyone at your job from totally hating you). Follow our basic tips for working like a Hot Chick and you'll be able to keep your career moving forward without missing out on any of the magical♥ heyday♥ moments that life has to offer.

# Twelve Trusty Tips
## for Business Behavior

We are constantly flabbergasted by the number of women we run into who talk about crazy shit at work, don't know how to act appropriately, or just flat out don't do their jobs—and don't seem to feel even the tiniest bit guilty about it. If you don't act right on the job, your paycheck and fun health benefits could be ripped out of your manicured hands faster than the planet's $CO_2$ levels are rising, but if you obey our top twelve trusty tips to basic office etiquette, we promise that you will move forward towards achieving your goals and balancing out your entire life without humiliating yourself or pissing off every single one of your colleagues. What more can a working girl ask for?

### Business Behavior #1: Perfect Punctuality

We know how much you hate the sound of your alarm clock and the fact that you might have to fight your three roommates (or even your husband) for the shower in the morning, but there is honestly no good excuse for being late. Get it together and come up with a plan that has you out of the shower, fighting the traffic, battling the long-ass Starbucks line, and walking into work at least five full minutes before you're expected to arrive.

### Business Behavior #2: Silence the Celly

Do you have any idea how annoying it is when you go to the bathroom and your cell phone rings (and rings and rings) with some catchy ring tone you downloaded when you should have been working? Your coworkers will remember exactly how much they hate you every time they find themselves humming that tune. Do yourself a favor and silence it before your colleagues try to use a silencer on you.

### Business Behavior #3: Quit Cursing

Don't even try calling us hypocrites. Curse words have their proper place, like Gordon Ramsay's mouth and funny books with the words "Hot Chick" in the title. They do not, however, belong in the workplace unless you're a porn star or a stand up comedienne like Kathy Griffin. Cursing at work instantly makes you appear as unprofessional and inelegant as the smell of last night's boxed white zinfandel on your breath, so censor yourself just a bit and you'll be glad that you did.

### Business Behavior #4: Prohibit Pilfering

No matter how underappreciated you may feel at work or how little time you have to go shopping, you do not have the right to sneak out a case of champagne or a new laptop when you think nobody's looking. How silly would you feel if you got fired over a desk chair? We hope you already know that this goes for stealing from your colleagues, too! Don't take their can of Diet Coke out of the communal fridge just because you're having a craving or "borrow" their corporate AmEx to buy those shoes on sale. Follow the golden rule ♥ and keep your hands to yourself, instead.

### Business Behavior #5: Keep Your Personal Life Private

We know that sometimes it can be more fun to chat about what's going on outside of work than it is to actually do work, but you need to limit how much of your private life you reveal at the office. You can speak generally about going on dates or planning your wedding, but don't waste your time (or theirs) boring your coworkers with the intimate details of your last one-night stand or stomach flu. The only reason they're listening is because they are getting paid to work next to you, but it's getting less and less worth it by the minute. Participate in idle chit chat for a few minutes a day, and then shut your mouth and get to work on what's really important—your job.

## Business Behavior #6: Prohibit Procrastination

The longer you procrastinate, the more the universe♥ will follow suit by taking its own sweet time to give you what you want in life. Making things like updating your Facebook status and checking the 70 percent off section of shopbop.com a higher priority than returning work emails or calling back a client may be what's preventing you from getting where you want in your career. You're not just hurting yourself by texting under your desk and uploading photos to Flikr instead of doing your job, either. You are unwittingly making your colleagues work that much harder to cover your ass, and they're starting to hate you. Do yourself a favor and prohibit procrastination before they turn on you faster than the hula-hoop-spinning hippo you've been busy watching on YouTube.

## Business Behavior #7: Give Yourself a Break

Come up for air every now and then and re-energize so that you can finish your job without breaking down from exhaustion. If you insist on eating lunch at your desk (even though we already told you not to), make sure to at least take a ten-minute walk to get some fresh air and much needed Vitamin D. If you're working late into the night, take an hour for yourself to meet a friend for a quick dinner or to run to the gym. But this doesn't mean that you should feel free to take long lunches or mid-afternoon trips to the mall on a regular basis. Work at least the minimum number of hours that are expected of you and you'll get out of the office and into your heyday♥ feeling much more productive and happy.

## Business Behavior #8: Don't Cry

It can be hard not to get emotional at work when you're under pressure and especially if it's that time of the month—heck, even Hillary Clinton got teary on the campaign trail! We know that a bad case of PMS can make it nearly impossible not to scream, cry, and break out into hysterics when the copier jams or your party of twelve leaves you a twelve-cent tip, but you must do everything in your power not to cry at work. It's sad but true that seeing you cry will make your boss respect you just a little less, so if you're going through something serious like an especially bad case of PMS, do yourself a favor and take a sick day.

## Business Behavior #9: Don't Cry Wolf

If you say your Grandma died and go to Bermuda for a week, what are you going to do when (G*d forbid) your grandmother really does die? Or if you tell your boss that crazy traffic made you late when you were really hung over, will anyone believe you when a tractor trailer really does overturn on the freeway? Be honest and don't be the Hot Chick who cried wolf or you will run the risk of losing the respect and trust of your colleagues, not to mention your job!

## Business Behavior #10: Avoid Annoying

From the doctor's office to the grocery store, there seems to be one incredibly annoying woman at every type of workplace. At our bank, it's the lady who snacks on peanuts, loudly giggles to her coworker about stupid shit, and flings her managerial key chain around with her acrylic nails so that we all know she's in charge. At our former job, it was the girl who microwaved the world's smelliest bag of popcorn every morning at 8:45 so that as soon as we arrived at work, we all became instantly nauseous. We're not saying that you have to ignore your own needs and become a people pleaser, but if you monitor how your actions affect others and try not to annoy the crap out of everyone who comes in contact with you, we promise you'll be better off.

## Business Behavior #11: Adjust Your Attitude

We want to slap the shit out of those of you in any sort of custumer service position who are judgmental, impatient, impolite, and flat out mean. You are not only making your own work life miserable with your bad attitude—you are making every client and coworker who has to deal with you suffer, too. Hate your job all you want, but stop taking it out on everyone around you or you will never be a true Hot Chick.

## Business Behavior #12: Do Your Job

You might be the CEO of a giant company or a college intern who is just flat out not doing your job. You know who you are. For some strange reason, you must think that you are better than your job. We wish we had the power to fire you and replace you with all those hard-working Hot Chicks who've gotten laid off, but just remember our friend karma. Every cheater eventually gets caught; if you don't start doing your job, we promise that the universe will make sure you get exactly what you deserve.

# *Organization Obligations*

We have constant fantasy sequences♥ about having perfectly organized closets and makeup bags and even being so damn organized that we don't need a junk drawer! But when it comes to
your work life, you can't let organization slide for one minute or
you'll end up with a worse case of OWL Syndrome♥ than the
Octomom's nanny. Staying organized is an obligation for every
woman who wants to get ahead in her career without feeling insane. Take the time to structure your work life with these five
tips and your whole existence will be more balanced and blissful.

### Create a Calendar

We don't care if you're sitting behind a desk all day crunching
numbers or running around a restaurant crunching tortilla chips
under your heels; you must have an organized calendar that maps
out your entire life in order to work like a Hot Chick. This doesn't
have to be complicated. Use an electronic calendar in Outlook or
Google if you're a tech-savvy Hot Chick, or go out every year and
buy a giant planner to write everything down in if you prefer pen
and paper. You are not Rain Man, so there is no way that your
brain can possibly remember everything. Don't kid yourself or test
yourself—just write that shit down and see how much less stressed
you feel.

*Trusty Tip: Don't defeat the purpose of having one place to organize
your time by having separate calendars for work and play. Instead,
use one calendar for everything and then color code it! Use one color
for personal events and another for work meetings to keep everything
together yet separate.*

## Do a To-Do

There are people out there who literally cannot do anything without writing it down and then crossing it off. These people may be going too far; we don't think you need to write down, "take a shower" or, "eat breakfast," but keeping everything that you need to do at work organized on one list will prevent you from forgetting any of them. Even if you have a magical♥ memory, this is a great way to free up some of that space in your mind. When you have nine million tasks swimming around in your head, writing them down will help you de-stress and focus. Plus, it's true that crossing things off the list feels almost as good as one of those bone-crunching Thai massages.

*Trusty Tip: When your to-do list is three pages long—like ours is right now—break it down into priorities and make mini to-do lists for each day. That way, looking at that long-ass list won't freak you out so much that it defeats the entire purpose of creating the list in order to stay sane and balanced.*

## Fabulous Filing

If you have a job where you receive literally five hundred emails a day, you need to file that shit or your brain might crash even sooner than your hard drive. Create a filing system for your emails and documents so that everything goes immediately into its proper place. If you have to search through all eight thousand emails in your inbox to get anything done, you're totally fucking up♥. Those of you who are lucky enough to not be bombarded by emails at work still need a filing system for your work. If your receipts, dental insurance claims, financial aid information, and sexual harassment packets are sitting on your desk in one giant pile, that chaos is definitely going to prevent you from working like a Hot Chick.

*Trusty Tip: Use the same sort of filing system for your personal life, too. Create a folder for all eight hundred emails about your best friend's bridal shower, make a file for all your car repair forms, and put all of your love letters in the same place. The peace of mind that comes with this type of organization can free up brain space for things that are much more fun.*

### Rule for Reminders

We don't want you to ever accidentally be late to your afternoon meeting, miss a business flight, or forget about that client who's holding on line one—so set reminders for yourself! Most electronic calendars (like Outlook and Google) have reminder settings so that you can bug yourself about things every fifteen minutes, every hour, or however often you need to. If you're not near a computer all day, then write down conference call times on your hand, set the alarm on your cell phone, or put a freaking egg timer in your bra. Life is nutty and it's easy to slip, so do whatever you need to do to remember everything that you have going on.

*Trusty Tip: This is especially important for all of you Hot Chicks who freelance or work from home. When you don't have a boss to remind you about that meeting or coworkers in your face to spark your memory, it's all on you to remember everything—so you really need to remember everything!*

### Savvy Scheduling

We know that many of you have jobs where the hours change every week and it feels like the shit is constantly hitting the fan because you have no structure or consistency to count on. In that case, it's up to you to create some sort of structure and consistency for yourself. Give yourself strict start times, breaks, and end times for your work or you might get distracted by shiny things, or forget to eat lunch and work for ten hours straight until you pass out and hit your head on the keyboard. Be your own boss and create a schedule that balances productivity with time to take care of your hot self!

*Trusty Tip:* *When you have an organized work schedule, it's much easier to fill in the rest of your time with the really important appointments like bikini waxes, spin classes, and dates with your girlfriends!*

# Email Etiquette

It's safe to say that email is now the number one way that we all communicate at work, and (like everything else in life) it has its pros and cons. We can do business with China without having to get on a plane and we can work from home when we're really tanning on the beach somewhere. It sure is convenient, but we think that email can sometimes be a bit too handy for its own good. It's just so easy to jot off a response and hit send without taking a moment to think through what you want to say. This can make you look extremely silly, and we want to make sure that you come across as well in your emails as you do in person, on the phone, and even via facsimile.

Email entered the world so quickly that we didn't really have a chance to prepare. We took typing classes in high school and learned how to write a proper business letter (oops, we're aging ourselves here), but there was no email class available or even any ground rules. We think it's time that somebody gave you working girls tips for sending professional, communicative emails that show you in your best light. Follow our dos and don'ts for email etiquette and set a good example for all of your coworkers who have been completely embarrassing themselves with their poor email behavior.

## Email Etiquette #1: Check Yourself

Seriously girls, how easy it is to hit that little spell check button before you hit send? It may soak up a whole thirty seconds of your day, but we think it is completely worth it to avoid coming across like a dyslexic three-year-old. Send all the typo-ridden, fucked up♥ emails you want to your girlfriends or your mom, but we think that business emails should be correct in their spelling and even their grammar. Take five minutes to learn the difference between "their," "there," and "they're" and you'll save yourself from looking like an idiot when it counts. We know, we know, there have been presidents who couldn't spell for shit, but unless you're in with the oil companies like them, we don't think you'll be getting ahead with emails that read like brainless gibberish.

### Email Etiquette #2: Finish Forwards

Do not ever (we mean ever, *ever*) forward a jokey, human interest, non-work email to your colleagues or G*d forbid your boss. This is the equivalent of sending an email to your entire company that says, "Right now I am wasting your money by sending stupid, frivolous emails instead of doing the job that you're paying me to do."

### Email Etiquette #3: Beware Blind Copy

Blind copying someone on an email is like whispering a secret to them, and it's easy for the person who was bcc'ed to not realize it and hit reply all, effectively spilling your secret and making everyone else who was on that email feel completely betrayed. The next time you're tempted to blind copy someone, leave them off the email and then forward your sent message to them. This way, they get the information you wanted them to see without the ability to blow your cover (and many of your working relationships right along with it).

### Email Etiquette #4: Address with Attention

Now that most email programs fill in the rest of the address after you type in the first letter, it's easier than ever to send your boss Martha Goldman an email that you meant to send to your friend Martha Garrison about your new favorite vibrator. You need to triple check that shit, ladies, and while you're at it, make sure that you didn't hit reply all to an email your work friend sent to the entire company and accidentally inform them all that you slept with the water cooler dude and he has a really small penis, and that's why you're not drinking water at work ever again. One tip to avoid these mistakes is to type out all of your emails with the "To" field blank and then—once your message is proofread and spell-checked—carefully type in the intended address. Though we've tried, we've never managed to successfully un-send an email, so pay meticulous attention before it's too late.

### Email Etiquette #5: Keep It from Being Personal

You need to keep your work email 100 percent separate from your personal email. We know how easy it is to jot off a note to your man or one of your friends from your work account, but please resist. Open your browser and log in to your personal account to send personal emails at work and it will be completely worth the extra twenty seconds of effort. This is a great way to keep your work and personal lives separate so that you can balance the two. Remember, your company has the right to monitor every email you send from their server. Do you really want them reading about the number of shots you did last night? Also, keeping the two email accounts apart makes it far more difficult for you to fuck up and mistakenly send an email meant for your boyfriend that says, "I can't wait to kiss you all over" to the nerdy guy in the IT department.

### Email Etiquette #6: Save Your Emails

Not to make you paranoid or anything, but keeping an email trail can be a very good thing if six months down the road someone dares accuse you of dropping the ball or never answering a question. It is so much fun in these instances to forward an old email proving that you're right with a simple note that says, "Please see below." Take the time to create an email filing system so that your incoming and outgoing messages are organized and at your pretty little fingertips at a moment's notice.

## Email Etiquette #7: Don't Use Abbreviations, Emoticons, or Other Stupid Shit

We know how dreary it can be to type out entire words. Gosh, it's so difficult. You really must, though, if you don't want to seem like a bratty teenager in your emails. Please refrain from using acronyms like OMG, WDYT, and especially LOL. You are not laughing out loud, nor should you be, about work matters. Also, stop putting smiley faces at the end of your sentences because you're afraid of coming across like (G*d forbid) a strong woman with an opinion. We still think it's better to be a strong woman at work than an LSE♥, hyper tween, which is how all those winky faces are making you seem. ☺

## Email Etiquette #8: Don't Over Email

If you need to send an email to ask a question or to get something done, then by all means send a clear, concise email, but please don't send a thousand unnecessary emails a day just to make yourself look busy or because you're bored. When you overload people's inboxes, they begin to dread the sight of your name and they also start taking your questions less seriously. Can you consolidate emails? Can you answer your own question with three more minutes of work? Can you get up, stretch your legs, and walk thirty feet to talk to the recipient in person? Prevent email from becoming your worst enemy by sending less of them.

## Email Etiquette #9: Watch Your Tone, Young Lady

It can be very hard to determine the intended tone of an email; that's why so many people rely on emoticons as if they're little electronic life jackets. Without using this crutch, you can make sure your emails don't sound unnecessarily bitchy by writing in complete, clear sentences, ending your emails with phrases like, "Thank you" and, most importantly, not sending emails when you're actually angry! It's so tempting to fire off a snarky response to your boss's backhanded compliment or your colleague's thirtieth braggy email about her daughter's SAT scores, but don't fall prey to this impulse. In fact, in these cases you're better off not responding at all. Roll your eyes to yourself, delete the email, and go on about your work so that your blood pressure will stay as balanced as your reputation.

**Email Etiquette #10: DON'T USE ALL CAPS!**
ISN'T THIS HARSH? DOESN'T IT FEEL LIKE WE ARE SCREAMING AT YOU? AND ISN'T IT EXTRA HARD TO READ? ARE YOU GETTING A HEADACHE RIGHT NOW TRYING TO READ THIS, LIKE A MIGRAINE SO BAD THAT YOU MIGHT JUST KILL YOURSELF?! WELL THEN PLEASE DO US ALL A FAVOR AND TURN OFF THAT CAPS LOCK BUTTON IF YOU WANT TO WORK LIKE A HOT CHICK (pretty please)!

# Hot Chicks *Do* Get
## the Corner Office
### (and the Penthouse Suite)

Much has been written on the subject of how women need to behave in the workplace in order to get ahead. Some say we have to strip ourselves of our femininity and act like men, while others believe we must become tough-as-nails bitches instead of sweet people pleasers. What we think is missing from this conversation (just like the exercise and diet conversation and the work/life conversation) is the message of balance. We think that in order to get ahead, you just need to act like a nice, feminine, confident woman—basically, just like our definition of a Hot Chick! If you started acting as unemotional and aggressive as a man, you would be completely denying who you are, and unless you're Chaz Bono, there is no reason to renounce your gender. On the other hand, you can't let emotions, PMS, or your desire to please others rule at work, either. You need to find a compromise between embracing your femininity and keeping your emotions at bay.

It's hard to know what amount of femininity will make you appear strong, confident, competent, and powerful without making other women jealous or giving all of the guys at work a boner. Many women tend to play small♥ at work and cover up every ounce of their femininity, but that is merely a form of self-denial that will only make you more LSE♥ in the long run, and as women are taking over the world little by little, there is no reason to pretend that we can't be girly and powerful at the same time. So if you've been trying to impersonate Donald Trump at work, stop it right now! Let yourself be a woman at work to the fullest extent of the word—the most confident, secure, passionate, organized, and authoritative woman that you can be.

Of course, there's also the issue of balance when it comes to being a pushover or acting like a bitch at work, and we have some bad news for you: if you act strong and confident at work and stand up for yourself, there are people out there who are going to call you a bitch no matter how kind and generous you actually may be. This is just a remnant of sexism that is still with us, and we hope you'll do your part by supporting your powerful female colleagues instead of resenting them. Then you must continue to help the cause by acting like a Hot Chick at work and ignoring those idiots who dislike you for it.

Listen to your intuition. There is a voice inside you that weeps when you let your boss stomp all over you and there is another one that calls you a giant asshole when you act condescending, bitchy, manipulative, or rude. Start paying close attention to how you react to workplace situations and adjust your attitude until you find the right balance between acting sweet and sickeningly sweet and between being powerful and becoming hostile. If you pay attention, you will know when you are not being your true self, your nicest self, or your most confident, Hot Chick self. Women are more intuitive than men, so use this to your advantage to become the woman you want to be, and trust that all of that goodness will come seeping out of your tiny pores the moment you start embracing the Hot Chick that you are and believing that you deserve the corner office, the penthouse suite, and all the other goodness that your heart could possibly desire.

# Chapter 5

## *Money Honey*

EVEN IN THE BEST ECONOMY, THE SUBJECT OF MONEY CAN BE AS MESSY AND COMPLICATED AS GOOD SEX, AND THE INFORMATION OUT THERE ABOUT HOW TO HANDLE YOUR MONEY IS AS CONTRA-DICTORY AS THE JUDGES' *AMERICAN IDOL* CRITIQUES. How are you supposed to work like a Hot Chick if you have no idea how to handle the money that you're working so hard to make? Well, we want you to find some balance when it comes to your money so that you can clock in and clock out with confidence in your cash!

Both men and women torture themselves over money matters. No matter how hard we work, it seems like there's never enough money to go around, and no matter how much we save, it feels like it all ends up going towards unpleasant things like dental work and taxes instead of vacations and new clothes. Finding a balance with money is obviously something that most of us aren't very good at, but the difference between men and women when it comes to money is that most women don't pay enough attention to it. Many of us think that it's unladylike or something to talk or learn about money, and we're scared to death by Suze Orman (who can blame us?), and so we remain as ignorant about finance as Paris Hilton is about Wal-Mart.

But you must take control of your finances if you want balance in your life. Financial problems can really take a toll on your stress level, your health, your job, and your marriage. Even if your money situation is halfway decent, the constant strain of trying to make ends meet can keep you from enjoying the simple things, prevent you from having a heyday ♥, and make your days at work feel worthless. So how do we strike the right balance when it comes to money matters? How do we learn to enjoy our lives when we are stressed to the max about today's bills, tomorrow's cash flow, and security in the unforeseeable future? Well, we're not financial experts or professional money managers (which right now is a good thing), but we have managed to find our own rules for spending, saving, and investing for the future without being driven insane by our unstable consumer culture. Follow our financial tips and before too long, you'll be in the money, honeys.

# Money Can't Buy Happiness

The majority of our world (and especially our country) is completely obsessed with spending and consuming. We're all sinking deeper into debt like it's quicksand, but at the same time we keep charging shit that we think will make us happy. It used to be that middle- and working-class people lived simple lives without too many fancy things, but now it seems like regular working folks have three homes and a flat screen in every room of each one. Of course it can be fun to buy things that are new, shiny, and smell like genuine leather, but once the initial excitement fades, does having these things actually make you a happier person? When you get into a fight with your best friend or find out that a family member is ill, do you say, "Well, who cares? I have all this great new stuff," or would you trade every single one of your possessions to get that friend back or make that family member well?

It's a cliché for a reason, and that reason is because it's true—money cannot buy happiness. If it could, would the world's richest and most famous celebrities be so self-destructive and miserable? Michael Jackson had more money than G*d and *was* a G*d to so many people, but his issues (whatever they were) couldn't be healed by endless wads of cash. Since we always tell you not to compare yourself to celebrities, think about someone you know. Maybe you know a Hot Chick who's rolling in dough but just found out she can't have children, or was a trust fund baby who got more love and affection from her accountant than she ever did from her parents. Don't be jealous of these people who have something that you want; instead, think about how many things you have that they would gladly give up every one of their dollars for.

It really is the people in your life and the good things that you do that will make your life feel complete, not the number of zeros at the end of your paycheck or your monthly bank statement. No matter how much you think a laser facial will change your life, nothing can compete with the things in this world that are free: the feeling of falling in love for the first time; being in awe of the planet when you're hiking alone in the wilderness; or just feeling completely comfortable and at home with the people you love most. Those are the things that make life truly worth living.

# But It Sure Does Help

Hold the phone, ladies; we're not idiots! We know that working so hard would feel much more worthwhile if your paycheck didn't disappear faster than an expensive spray tan, and your heyday♥ might be a lot more fun if you had a cute Juicy wallet full of cash to spend and an equally juicy savings account to use as back up. It's hard to stay balanced and happy when you can't afford to take a yoga class with your girlfriends on your precious day off, go on vacation with your husband, or buy a pair of magic♥ jeans for your date with a new beau. However, it's a whole lot worse when you can't afford medical insurance or a week's worth of groceries. There's a difference between not being able to afford luxuries and struggling to have necessities, and we hope you recognize it.

Spending money is just like eating chocolate cake. If you choose to splurge on special occasions, you will appreciate it more and will never feel deprived—but if you indulge too often, it won't satisfy you anymore, and will start to make you feel like shit (ironically enough). You have to find that happy medium between over-consuming to the point where you're drowning and miserable, and consuming just enough that you feel joyful and lucky. You have to learn how to stop yourself from charging things on your credit card that you *think* will make you happy so that you're able to spend money on the things that really will be worth it. Maybe that means not buying any new clothes for a year and then splurging on a fabulous honeymoon, or cooking dinners at home and bringing leftovers for lunch and then surprising your mother with a sixtieth birthday party at a five-star restaurant. The memories of your honeymoon and the grateful look on your mother's face will be worth a lot more than the crap you barely remember eating every week at The Cheesecake Factory or the ten pairs of new jeans that are now shoved in the back of your closet, and that is the kind of financial balance that we want you to have.

Being balanced about money is not just about spending and saving the right amount. It's about seeing money for what it is—a tool. Money in and of itself won't make you happy, but if you use it in an intelligent and well-planned way, it *can* help make you happy. This is an incredibly important lesson, and one that you often learn from struggling with money. If you always have a giant safety net of cash beneath you, you will probably never learn how to appreciate, respect, and properly use money in a way that truly makes you happy. But if you have to struggle and fight for your money and drive a car that's held together with duct tape and bungee cords, you will be more likely to learn how to use your money strategically on things that will actually make you happy.

# *Money Matters*

It's time for us to give you gorgeous gals some tried and true tips that will help you use your money to live like the Hot Chicks that you are! Follow our rules to M-O-N-E-Y and find that financial balance that will keep you from wanting to slit your pretty little wrists. We can't promise overnight prosperity like our horoscope keeps teasing us with, but having a money plan is always better than not having one. Even if you lose everything, you can at least go down in debt knowing that you tried.

### M—Make a Plan
Sometimes it's easier to just ignore a problem rather than look at it head on. That's why so many of us end up staying in bad relationships, dead-end jobs, and roach-infested apartments far longer than we should. In all three cases, ignoring the problem always ends up making it worse, so it's time to face the music (and the numbers) and make a real life budget for yourself. Write down how much you make each month (after taxes, please!) and weigh it against all of your expenses, from rent and utilities to eating out and going shopping. Be honest about how much you spend! If you find that you're spending more than you're earning, start making cuts until the balance is on the other side and then start to live according to your budget. It may be hard to see your grim financial matters in black and white, but at least you'll be empowered with the facts and therefore able to change them. Be confident about the fact that you are taking control of your life like the Hot Chick that you are.

*Money Maker: Embrace technology and create your budget on a gi- ant spreadsheet or a program like QuickBooks that will do all the math for you. Treat your budget like a garden—spend time caring for and nurturing it and it will pay you back in the long run!*

## O—Organize It

You know how good it feels when your closet is all color-coded and your shoes are organized by heel height? It makes getting dressed in the morning so much easier when you don't have to search under your bed and then through piles of dirty panties to find a lost shoe. Well, the same is true for your cashola! The best way to arrange your money is to have it in different accounts for specific purposes. You should have a checking account that should be balanced with your budget, a savings account for short-term heyday stuff like weekend trips and shopping sprees, and a long-term savings account for retirement, major purchases, or emergencies. Even if you don't think you have one extra penny to save each month, we want you to put this book down (at the end of this chapter), go to the bank, and open a freaking savings account! Even if you only put five dollars in there each week it's better than nothing, but you should make it a priority to squirrel 5 or 10 percent of your income away each month. It'll be exciting to see your money grow over time, and you'll receive immediate gratification from having your money all organized and happy in its proper place.

*Money Maker: Organize your spending money and grocery money in little envelopes that fit nicely in your purse and pay in cash as much as possible so that you don't go over budget when you're tempted by all sorts of nonsense at Target or a million unnecessary treats at Trader Joe's.*

## N—Never Be Irresponsible

Sorry, ladies, but it is totally irresponsible to spend more money than you bring in each month. Unless you're going through a momentary setback (a layoff or an emergency of some sort), there is no excuse for this. Don't be scared, though; you just need to cut out some frills so you can gain some thrills. Think about what's really important. Did your grandparents need new jet skis and highlights every month, or did they work hard to put food on the table and take pleasure in sitting at that table together each night? Take a note from your forefathers (and foremothers, thank you very much) and see how much you can easily cut from your monthly budget. Of course, being responsible and living within your budget means avoiding that dreaded credit card debt at all costs. Stop living in fantasyland and denying the fact that you probably won't be able to pay off your balance in a year when your interest rates go through the roof! Even if you start making more money, your bills will likely grow along with your salary, and once you start the cycle of debt it will never end.

*Money Maker: Do whatever you have to do to avoid getting into credit card debt—cut up your credit cards and live off cash, or lock your cards in a safe and use them only for emergencies (and no, massages and sales at Barney's do not count as emergencies).*

### E—Educate Yourself

You Hot Chicks have to take money matters into your own little hands and start educating yourselves! If you don't know the difference between a regular IRA, a Roth IRA, a 401(k), and a pension, you need to learn now. Remaining in the dark about your finances makes it much easier for you to let them get out of control or for someone to take advantage of you. Once you learn the basics it won't feel so scary, and you will feel much more powerful—so stop putting this off! If you're not quite sure how social security works you don't need to worry, because neither does our government, but start researching different types of investments so that you know the difference between a Britney Spears CD and the type of CD you put your money in and the distinction between good debt (low-interest student loans and mortgages) and bad debt (a wallet full of credit cards from Macy's, Sears, and Victoria's Secret that you only pay the minimums on every month). Remember that the rich get richer by knowing everything there is to know about their money, so even if you're not rich now, you can get a little bit closer by learning about yours.

*Money Maker: If you work for a company with a benefits or HR department, schedule a meeting with them right now to learn about 401(k)s, stock options, flexible spending accounts, and all sorts of good money stuff.*

### Y—You Can Do It

Good news, ladies—you have the power to get your finances in order and to create abundance in your life. You have the tools, the smarts, and the ability, and soon you'll have the knowledge to use your money for whatever you decide is most important. It may sound cheesy, but if you put good energy out, you'll get good things back. That goes for love and friendship, and it goes for money, too. So stop saying things like, "I'm broke," or feeling like you're doomed to live paycheck to paycheck for the rest of your life. Once you follow these steps and create a budget and a plan, cut the nonsense spending, and get schooled on the ways of money, you can sit back and trust that the universe♥ will take care of the rest. If you are doing good work and putting out good vibes, you will get good things in return. It may take time and it may not come in the crazy proportions you have fantasy sequences♥ about, but by taking control of your money, you will end up with fewer financial problems.

*Money Maker: If you really need to start making more money, sit down and make a list of things you can do immediately and in the long term to make extra cash. If you make sure these are positive and productive and take the appropriate steps to make them happen, the universe♥ will respond with money.*

# The Beauty of Abundance

It's funny how so many of us (and we are guilty of this, too) focus on what we don't have instead of what we *do* have, or worry about what might go wrong instead of having fantasy sequences ♥ about what could go right. It's the classic "martini glass half empty" scenario. If you constantly think and complain about not having enough, the universe ♥ will continue to give that to you—but if you flip the switch and concentrate on the abundance that you already have, the universe ♥ will continue to supply you with abundance.

We know you might be thinking, *How the hell am I supposed to focus on my "abundance" when I have six kids and three jobs and I'm still barely making ends meet?* Well, as hard as it may be, you can think of something that you are grateful for in your life, and we want you to put more energy there. Say to yourself, "I am grateful to have a beautiful, healthy family, and I know that the universe ♥ will help me provide for them" when you're lying in bed at night, instead of worrying about what will happen if you lose your job tomorrow. Think about all of the things you are lucky to have, even if it's simply a warm roof over your head, a bounty of available food and people who love you. You can focus on superficial things if you want to. Express gratitude for your grandmother's antique jewelry, your wedding ring, or the fact that you were finally able to buy your own home.

Have you ever met a girl who is just a total train wreck and can never seem to get a break, is always broke and heartbroken, and keeps getting into car accidents and catching weird STDs? Well, have you ever noticed that these are usually the same women who are always blaming everyone else in the world for their problems and complaining about how life is unfair? Then there are the Hot Chicks who have their shit together and walk around exuding confidence and happiness. Even if they don't have that much money, they've managed to make the best spiked lemonade out of the lemons that life has given them. You may think this is a chicken or egg situation (did the circumstances create the outlook, or vice versa?), but we are pretty sure that the Hot Chick who feels blessed and focuses on the abundance in her life, who looks in the mirror and is grateful for her beauty instead of bitter about her flaws, is the woman who will live the most fulfilling life in every sense of the word.

The more you open your eyes to the beauty and abundance that surrounds you, the more well-being and comfort the universe♥ will provide. Think about the things in your life that drive you nuts and pay attention to yourself when you start complaining. Instead of blaming your asshole boss for not giving you a raise, tell the universe♥ that you already have everything you need. And instead of worrying about what the future might hold, imagine a bright, shiny, gorgeous future for yourself. You deserve to have everything you want (within reason!)—and you will begin to receive it as soon as you start to value what you already have.

# Saving for Your Heyday ♥

There will always be bills and boring necessities that you have to spend money on, and we sincerely hope that you prioritize your paychecks to pay for things like rent, gas, and utility bills. But life isn't all about work, and neither is money, so we want to help you find ways to finance your play time as well as the rest of your life. These small ways of cutting cash corners will add up to a bounty of bucks for you to spend on whatever fun splurges you choose.

### 1—Strategically Schedule Shopping
Use your friends to curtail your shopping habit just like you use them to help you follow your diet and your exercise plan. Make a rule with a girlfriend that you'll go shopping together for the summer in May and only spend a certain amount, and then you are not allowed to even walk into a mall or click on an online shopping site until September. Hold each other accountable. You can do this in reverse, too, and plan ahead to buy new things only during end of season sales. If your winter coat is molting in January, wait until February—when all of the coats are 50 percent off—to buy a new one. If you schedule it right and use a little bit of self-control, you'll be able to buy twice as much with the same amount of money.

### 2—Eat Out Instead of Ordering In
We've found that the best way to afford amazing meals out is to be super frugal with food the rest of the time. It's a waste of money to buy expensive take-out meals or fancy Whole Foods fare only to devour it in front of the TV. A hundred dollars spent on groceries will last approximately four times longer than the same amount spent on takeout, and then you can use that extra cash to go to fun happy hours and occasionally to fancy restaurants. Those spe-

cial occasions will be so much more memorable and celebratory than boxed meals eaten on the couch, so see how far you can stretch your grocery bill by buying the generic brand of peanut butter, whatever produce is on sale, and only as much food each week as you will actually eat! If you are throwing rotten food out of your fridge every weekend, then you might as well pour ketchup on your twenty-dollar bills and eat those. Stop wasting money on literal garbage that you could have spent on a pedicure, brunch with a girlfriend, or two and a half martinis.

### 3—Cut (or Print) Coupons

If she was smart, your mom probably sat on the couch watching M\*A\*S\*H cutting coupons for laundry detergent and paper towels. Well, just because M\*A\*S\*H has been off the air for years and the days of cutting coupons out of the newspaper are over, that doesn't mean that coupons themselves aren't still worthwhile. You can go to www.valpak.com, enter your zip code, and print coupons for all sorts of local deals; check out www.coolsavings.com for savings on everything from groceries to auto repairs; and go to www.groupon.com to get a daily coupon for local restaurants and spas. Instead of spending money by shopping online, make yourself some spending money with these online deals!

### 4—Sample Some Sales

Once again, if you don't buy things at full price, you can either buy more or use all of the money you save on something else. Sample sales are ideal for saving major bucks on everything from office basics to wedding gowns. Web sites like Daily Candy and Top Button list local sample sales around the country, and now there are even online samples sales for those of you who don't live in major cities with their own in-person sales! Rue La La and Gilt are two of our favorite places online to score designer clothes at up to 80 or 90 percent off! Be extra smart and buy birthday or Christmas gifts when you find an exceptionally good deal, and you'll have more money to spend on your own killer New Year's outfit.

## 5—Benefit from Bonuses

We don't want you to ever buy something at a department store makeup counter without getting a bag full of bonus goodies. If you are going to spend fifty bucks on a new eye cream, please help yourself justify that expense by getting a cute bag with a lipstick, mini moisturizer, and travel-sized mascara, too. Chances are that new eye cream isn't going to do shit for your wrinkles, so you might as well squeeze a little more fun out of it, right? You can also save the bonus stuff for stocking stuffers, tie it on top of birthday gifts, or give it to your little sister as her own little heyday♥ bonus.

## 6—Bask in Money Back

Please make sure to read the fine print to check that you're not signing away your firstborn or 10 percent of your annual income in exchange, but if you do this correctly, your favorite restaurants and hotels will actually give you money back just for being there! Many credit card companies also offer cash back bonuses every time you use their cards. We encourage you to take advantage of this, but only if you can control yourself and only charge what you can actually afford. Paying 20 percent APR on a five-thousand-dollar purchase just to get 2 percent cash back does not make a whole lot of sense, and we really hope you know that by now.

## 7—Cut Out the Negative

We know that most of you probably have at least one habit that is costing you money and is also bad for you. Is it a daily venti frappuccino with whipped cream, a twice a day bubble tea addiction, or a daily pack of cigarettes? Identify whatever your one vice is and calculate how much it is costing you. For example, the frappuccino habit costs about five dollars a day, which adds up to over eighteen hundred dollars a year. Staggering, isn't it? Add a flavor shot and we're talking about well over two grand and two hundred thousand calories a year just for a caffeine boost. Cut out one thing that's as bad for your bod as it is for your wallet and they'll both be better off.

## 8—Free Is Fabulous
The next time that semi-cute guy in front of the movie theater asks if you want tickets to a free screening, don't just say no out of habit. It's fun to see a random movie for free on a Tuesday night! Sure, the film might suck, and the line might suck even harder, but you'll be out in the world doing something interesting and even have enough money for some of that ridiculously overpriced popcorn. Always be on the lookout for things like free delivery, buy one get one free sales, free breadsticks with your pizza, or a Macy's free shipping sale the next time you have to buy someone a wedding present. (Remember, you have a year.) They say there's no such thing as a free lunch, but we say doing the research to get these free extras is even better.

## 9—Work Your Job
We bet the company you work for has all sorts of employee discounts and benefits you don't even know about. We just got 17 percent off of our monthly Verizon bill just by showing our company ID card, and you can probably do something similar! Many companies also have arrangements with local museums and galleries for discounted (or even free) admission, and some even have partnerships with mortgage brokers for discounted housing

fees! Spend some time on your company's Web site and grilling the chicks in HR, and soon you'll have more money to spend on things that are more fun.

**10—Avoid Fees**

Do you want to pay good money and get absolutely nothing in return? We didn't think so! Make sure you're not doing any stupid shit like taking out money from other banks' ATMs, paying for your checking account, getting charged per text, or getting slapped with any other nonsense fees. Your bank and credit card companies can hit you extra hard when you're traveling, so before going abroad, get a Capital One card (the only one that doesn't charge an extra 3 percent for every international transaction) and make sure that you never have to take a cash advance out on your credit card. Right now you might be paying hundreds of extra dollars in little chunks that you don't even notice, so pay attention and don't be afraid to ask questions and negotiate when you see a suspicious fee arise.

# Chapter 6

## *Working Wardrobe*

WHILE WE HOT CHICKS HAVE MANY MORE OPTIONS
THAN MEN, IT'S ALSO A LOT MORE DIFFICULT TO FIND
AN APPROPRIATE WORKING WARDROBE THAT IS AT
ONCE SUITABLE FOR YOUR JOB, AUTHORITATIVE, AND
FEMININE. There seem to be two routes here: either strip yourself of your sexuality and dress like a man in unflattering pants
suits and loafers or embrace your femininity in a flattering dress
and heels and risk not being taken seriously. Of course, working
like a Hot Chick means finding a way to be sexy and womanly
without looking (and feeling) too vulnerable and exposed. You
can dress as sloppily or sluttily as you want on the weekends (as
long as you're comfortable with people viewing you that way), but
the way you present yourself at work really is important. If you
wear wrinkled, stained clothes, people will assume that you are
also sloppy about your job; if you wear a three-inch skirt with six-

inch heels, people will assume that you have no brains and need to sleep your way to the top.

There are all sorts of different jobs with all sorts of different dress codes, but unless you're a stripper or an actress playing a stripper, you need to show up at work looking neat, clean, and professional. In this chapter, we are going to guide you through this challenge with a list of clothing basics that every Hot Chick should have in her working wardrobe, teach you how to use your assets without looking like a whore, and give you an all-important laundry list of clothing items that should never see the fluorescent lights of the office during the day.

# The ABCs of
# What to Wear

Some women think that paying attention to their clothing is a frivolous waste of time and money, while others are total shopaholics who use work as an excuse to spend countless hours and thousands of dollars to create their dream wardrobes. Well, we think that the perfect balance is somewhere between looking like a crusty homeless woman and being mistaken for Carrie Bradshaw. What makes you feel sexy and powerful can vary from Hot Chick to Hot Chick. Some of us feel fabulous in organic cotton while others shine when our accessories all match; we want you to figure out what works for you and wear it with pride.

You may think that what you wear to work doesn't matter, especially if you don't interact with clients or attend meetings on a daily basis, but it does. You can't show up to work looking like a sloppy, slutty, dirty, mismatched mess and expect to get ahead. It's not true that the girl with the cutest shoes wins, but the girl who is the most poised and comfortable in her skin (and in her shoes) does. Follow these three simple steps and you will feel and look like a Hot Chick at every employee meeting, each business conference, and even when you're just typing away at your desk.

## A—Always Appropriate
Conventional wisdom says to dress for the job you want instead of the job you have, and we agree with that—unless you're secretly vying for a slot on *Survivor*. Look at what your boss is wearing and what her boss is wearing and find something that suits your personality from the same part of the formality spectrum. You probably already know not to wear jeans if everyone else is wearing a

suit, but you also shouldn't wear a suit if you work in a place where everyone else is wearing jeans. No matter what the dress code is at your workplace, you need to find a way to fit into it while looking polished, pulled together, and classy. Of course, the industry you work in will determine exactly what is appropriate, but here are some guidelines that work for every job (at least the ones with daytime working hours).

You do not have to apologize for or cover up your womanly body, but if pickles from your sandwich fall into your bra at lunch, your shirt is too low cut. If you can't bend over to pick up a pencil without getting nervous about your tampon string showing, then that skirt is too short. A formerly white button-down shirt that is now a strange grayish color, yellowed around the armpits, and nubby from too many washings should be used exclusively as a dust rag. Any item with a hole in it of any size is not suitable for work (and yes, that includes jeans). Go through your closet and put everything you own that is "appropriate" for work in its own little section, and if in the end that section is empty, don't worry! Just use our shopping list below, drop one hundred dollars at Target, and you'll be good to go until your next raise.

### B—Balance Beauty

We spent many years covering every inch of ourselves at work because we felt LSE♥ about our bodies and thought that it was safer to dress as boring as possible to avoid getting the wrong kind of attention for being too sexy. Then one day we realized that we were playing small♥, and that we had every right to feel fabulous and sensual at work—but of course we had to be very careful not to let it all hang out, either. We want to help you find a balance in your working wardrobe so that Kathie Lee never makes fun of *your* cleavage on national television. The trick is to have items in your closet that balance your personality with what is appropriate for work. Don't hide or change your personality in order to look exactly like all the other office drones, but find a happy medium between your work self and your play self.

The first step is to make sure that your work clothes fit you well. Don't be afraid to wear things that accentuate your curvy hips, toned legs, or your perky bust line. When professional clothes fit you well they can be extremely flattering, and balancing worky style with a cut that makes you feel feminine is key. You can have the most professional pants on the planet, but if they are sagging in the ass and dragging on the floor, you're not going to look sharp or feel fierce at the office. We know that tailors can be obnoxiously expensive, so find a brand that fits and flatters your figure and invest in a few key pieces that you'll always be able to count on.

Second, focus on the details that will let your personality shine through your otherwise humdrum office outfits. Pair plain work pants with a funky belt that gives you just a bit of edge, or dare to wear a killer pair of heels with a corporate-looking suit. Spice yourself up with accessories that make you feel pretty. A dangly pair of earrings or fun patterned tights can make you feel fabulous and sexy while always staying professional. Finally, balance your wardrobe by mixing it up and wearing things that wouldn't ordinarily go together. This is an especially good tip for those occasions when you have a board meeting at four, a blind date at six, and no time to change in between. Throw on a sexy camisole underneath a blazer and then take the blazer off if the guy turns out to be cute, or wear a menswear-type vest over a bright top with a pair of skinny pants and heels. If you add subtle elements of sexiness to your mundane, everyday basics, you will have found the perfect balance for your boardroom beauty.

## C—Color = Classy

If you're the kind of girl who gets as excited about khaki pants from the GAP as we do about Godiva chocolate, then we might have a hard time getting you to wear a bright red suit, but we do want to stress the importance of color. Color is proven to enhance moods, so wearing brights at work will not only make you happier but also cheer up everyone at work who comes in contact with you. Wearing color is also a sign of confidence, so one look at your emerald green blouse and everyone will instantly know that you are a self-assured Hot Chick. If you cover up in head to toe black, brown, or grey, you'll be a whole lot easier to ignore, and if people don't look at you, how will they notice that you're the one who should be getting ahead instead of all those other girls? Don't ever be afraid to stand out and call attention to yourself—adding a rainbow of colorful clothes to your closet is a classy way to do so. Let your confidence shine through with dazzling hues of color, and both your mood and your future will suddenly start to look a whole lot brighter.

# Laundry List for Leading Ladies

Now that you've got some basic rules down, it's time to go shopping for these ten items that every working girl must have in her closet for interviews, meetings, and of course every day on the job. Now, if you work at Sea World or your dream is to be porn star (girl, we need to chat), then you can skip this part, but for roughly 99 percent of you, owning these ten essential pieces will ensure success and severely cut down on your monthly number of "I have nothing to wear" meltdowns.

## 1—Savvy Suits

Even if you work at Hot Topic and think you will never wear a suit in this lifetime, you should still go out and buy at least two of them. They are critical for interviews and you can make them suitable (get it?) for every day wear by pairing the blazer from one suit with a plain pair of pants or the skirt from another suit with a silk button-down or another casually cute top. If you have an old suit in your closet already, just make sure it still zips and that you can close the jacket without the buttons popping off in the middle of a meeting.

## 2—Basic Button-Downs

Make sure you at least have one black and one white button-down shirt to wear with fun vests and scarves, and one colored one to pair with black pants. They should fit you well so that you can move without the buttons pulling and showing everyone your belly button ring. You can mix it up and buy them in silky fabrics, but we think there's something dead sexy about a woman in a classic, crisp white button-down.

### 3—Mullet Shoes

These are like the hairstyle, but much more stylish because they are shoes that are all work in the front, but a party in the back. You know what we mean—close-toed, conservative loafer types with a surprising sassy platform or sexy high heel. These are an essential heyday♥ item because they can help you look right for work but still feel hot at happy hour.

### 4—Daytime Dresses

When you wear a dress, you only have one item of clothing to worry about and it's so easy to look put together by just throwing one on with tights and a cute pair of shoes. Of course, halters, sundresses, and strapless numbers are out of the question for work unless you run an oceanfront café or something, but wrap dresses and sweater dresses are especially good for office jobs because they are professional, flattering, and comfortable. Make sure you have at least one of each and see how much more productive you feel the next time you play "dress" up.

### 5—Tight Pants

We don't want your pants to be so tight that your coworkers can see the picture on your work ID through your back pocket, but you shouldn't feel like you have to wear horribly baggy, pleated pants to work, either. Pull out those black pants that you wore clubbing ten years ago when tight black pants were the shit and try them on with a button-down shirt. They flatter your post-butt-class♥ derrière without looking too hoochie and are perfect for your job, right? Whether you're a bartender or a technician, you should get pairs in black, grey, and brown so that your ass will feel hot as you work it.

### 6—Seductive Sweaters

Wearing sweaters to work in the winter can make you feel cozy, warm, and sexy because there's just something about the way a fine-knit sweater hugs your womanly curves without showing any skin that drives men wild. Make sure you have a couple of form-fitting ones and a few roomier ones that give you room to breathe on days when you're feeling bloated or ate way too much Mexican food the night before.

### 7—Lacy Lingerie

Lingerie is inappropriate for work, right? Well, as long as you wear it *underneath* your clothing, you're wrong. Secretly wearing luscious unmentionables where no one else can see them will make you feel sexy and passionate all day long. It will give you a seductive sparkle to your eye that will capture everyone's attention and help you be your most confident Hot Chick self. (Plus, you never know who you're going to meet after work.)

### 8—Pearl Necklace

Unless you're Jenna Jameson, we don't mean that kind. We are talking about a long, luxurious strand of pearls that you can layer around your pretty neck or wrap around your wrist to make even the most boring work outfits instantly classy, sexy, and beautiful. They don't have to be real pearls, either. Unless you're a gemologist, your coworkers won't know the difference between a strand that's worth three grand and one that cost three bucks at Accessories Galore.

## 9—Sophisticated Scarves

These add a pop of color and European *je ne sais quoi* to even the most boring work outfit on the planet and are essential for covering up hickeys or curling iron burns that just look like hickeys. (Sure, we believe you.) Don't be afraid; just tie one around your pretty neck and see how fabulous you feel.

## 10—Magic ♥ Jeans

For casual Fridays only, you should have one pair of jeans that fits you perfectly, reveals no muffin top, thong string, or ass crack, makes your butt feel perkier, helps your legs look longer, and generally makes you feel like the hottest Hot Chick to ever type a memo. Finding the right pair of magic ♥ jeans can mean an investment of time as well as money, but it's like finding your soul mate—the search may be long and painful, but you'll know when it's right and it will all have been worth it!

# Dirty Laundry

If you wear these things to work, you are being self-destructive and preventing yourself from feeling like a Hot Chick and getting ahead. Is it a cry for help? Are you still feeling too LSE♥ to let your true beauty shine at your job? Whatever the reason is, toss these items into a "weekends only" sack or you may end up getting sacked yourself.

### 1—Mants
"Mants" stands for "man pants" and they are (duh) pants that a man would wear. We had a job once where we were forced to wear brown polyester mants every day, and it took us years to recover. Do yourself a favor and stop hiding your girlish figure in loose, pleated, horrible mants. Even the word sounds ugly.

### 2—Sweats
Unless you are an Olympic athlete or design clothing for Juicy Couture (hey, can you send us some stuff?), you must never wear sweats to work, not even the cute terry kind with fun words across the butt. (*Especially* that kind.) The rest of the world has to actually get dressed in the morning, and guess what? So do you.

### 3—Pleather
We see those new pleather leggings everywhere, but we had better not see them on you at work unless you are employed at a sex shop or as a dominatrix. If you can wash your pants with Windex, they are not appropriate for work.

### 4—Sparkles

If you're not a stripper or a contestant on *Dancing with the Stars*, you should not have sequins on your work clothes or glitter all over your body. Business and the BeDazzler don't mix!

### 5—Sneaks

If you teach Phys Ed or coach cheerleaders we'll allow it, but otherwise, only break out those kicks at the gym. And we're really sorry, but please don't ever do that horrible '80s career woman commuter thing and show up to work wearing white sneakers and slouchy socks over your pantyhose. Nobody will be able to take you seriously after that.

### 6—Overdone Accessories

No hoop earrings that your puppy could jump though, no leather chokers with spikes unless you're a body piercer at a tattoo shop, and please, ladies, one or two rings are fine, but when we see women typing emails with chunky, tarnished gold rings on every single freaking finger, it completely grosses us out.

### 7—Lingerie Lookalikes

Keep the racy stuff underneath your clothing, ladies, and stop wearing anything that could be mistaken for lingerie at work. No skirts that might actually be slips, no dresses that could pass for nighties, and no slinky tops that look like they're from Fredericks of Hollywood. This also includes anything sheer or that slides off your shoulders. Your boss does not need to know what color bra you're wearing—even if he wants to.

### 8—Tubes and Tanks

Tank tops are perfect for just about every occasion other than work, so you already have plenty of opportunities to wear them.

Tube tops, on the other hand, mystify us on a daily basis, but especially when we see them at work. They're restricting, uncomfortable, and flatter no one, so think twice before ever wearing one, and think about a hundred times before wearing one to work.

### 9—Flip-Flops

We don't care how hot it is outside. Really, we don't. You can work in an un-air-conditioned office in New Orleans in the middle of August and you'll still look ridiculous wearing flip-flops to work (unless you're a lifeguard or own a surf shop). Have some self-respect and put on actual shoes so that you don't risk grossing anyone out with your fucked up ♥ pinky toe that looks like a penguin.

### 10—Stripper Gear

Save the fishnets and leopard print stilettos for Halloween or your honeymoon, but don't step one foot into your office with them on. Also, don't let yourself become a cliché by looking cheap in chipped red nail polish or acrylics that are so long you could dig your own grave in less than five minutes. Keep it classy, ladies, and you'll look a lot more competent.

# How Much Is Too Much?

**The Cleavage Conundrum**

Somewhere between 1950s housewives, the power bitches of the '80s, and today's post-femininity, cleavage has become a sort of taboo in the workplace and we don't think that's fair. We are women and we have breasts, and it can be extremely difficult and disheartening to spend all day covering them up, squishing them down, and generally trying to pretend that they don't exist. Of course, there are certain necklines that are simply inappropriate for work (like anything that J-Lo might wear to the Grammys), so we want to make sure you know the difference between professional cleavage and slutty cleavage.

Professional cleavage is a wrap dress that lies just an inch or less under your natural boob line or a button-down with the top button undone. Slutty cleavage includes anything that is both tight and low cut, shows any amount whatsoever of side boob, or simply reveals more than one inch of definite cleavage. What can be confusing is the fact that slutty cleavage also includes instances when there isn't any actual cleavage visible, but the fit of the top is so poor that there is a double boob effect going on or you can see the outline of the push-up gel pad in your Victoria's Secret water bra underneath your shirt.

On the other hand, some people say that any amount of cleavage is inappropriate at work, that it detracts from others seeing you as a professional and causes them to view you strictly as a sex object. Well, we disagree with these people. Men are allowed to be men at work. They are encouraged to be tough and to use their height and muscles to get what they want. We want to be allowed to be women at work, too. No, you shouldn't manipulatively use your bust line to flirt or sleep your way to the top, but why shouldn't you be allowed to go to work every day looking and feeling like a woman, without having to hide the fact that you are, in fact, a woman with a sexy, powerful, beautiful body? We want you to wear whatever makes you feel your absolute best, whether that's a turtleneck up to your ears or a dress that shows off your killer décolletage. We want you to look at the sexy, strong women in other countries who are running major portions of the world and go to work with the very same liberated sensuality, passion, and professionalism as they do.

# Chapter 7

## *Business Booty*

NO MATTER HOW HARD WE TRY TO FIGHT IT, SOME-
TIMES LOVE AND WORK CAN GET AS TANGLED UP AS
OUR SHEETS ON A WARM SUNDAY MORNING. They say not
to shit where you eat, which is just gross, and not to mix business
with pleasure—but the truth is that infusing your work life with a
bit of office recreation can be extremely exciting. There's nothing
like showing up to work with butterflies in your tummy because
you're going to see the guy who twitterpates♥ you at the ten a.m.
meeting to get your blood flowing, and it's that very exhilarating
illicitness that makes business booty so electrifying. Daydreaming
about getting some kisses from the cute assistant in the broom
closet can keep you feeling perky and positive, not to mention
make those ten-hour workdays pass by in a flash. Ladies, we've
been there. We've had everything from crushes to full-blown relationships with men at work, and we've learned something in the

process; they cause a lot of drama and stress, but once in a while they're actually worth it.

When choosing to engage in some business booty, you have to be extremely careful not to let it mess with your head at work and sabotage your success. Some things are obviously bad ideas, like having a one-night stand with your officemate, sleeping with your boss in hopes of getting a raise, or doing the walk of shame back to work wearing the same rumpled outfit as the day before. All of these things can leave you so preoccupied by your workplace romance that you forget it's called a workplace for a reason. Before you know it, you're having emotional breakdowns in the break room and getting caught on the conference table with your pants down. Well, don't worry because we can teach you how to mix business with pleasure and always come out on top (or in whatever position you prefer).

# You Deserve Love, but Not on the Clock

This chapter is not about love; it's about how mixing your work life and your love life can be more intoxicating and destructive than combining Long Island Iced Teas with red wine. Merging two parts of your life that should be separate, like work and love (or sex and food; we've never understood that one) will most certainly keep you from living like a Hot Chick by making you feel out of whack and unbalanced.

It's really hard sometimes to stop from getting mixed up with some hottie at your job, especially if you spend the majority of your life at work. Who has time to meet guys outside of work when there is a plethora of penises greeting you at nine a.m. every morning? They're all so cute and freshly showered, their belts and shoes actually match, and you know how they take their coffee and what they eat for lunch—so of course you can't help but wonder what they're doing when they close their office doors or step outside to take a personal call. You get to know these dudes so well that you can tell when they've gotten lots of sleep or no sleep—or even if they've gotten laid! This makes it very hard to not obsess over the men you work with, but if you want love in your life, you are going to have to find it somewhere else.

This is your job, and you need that job to pay your bills and move forward in your career. Why would you want to risk your job just to get a date when there are guys who you don't work with all over the freaking place? Spend some time outside of work looking for love and focus on your job while you're at the office, because it is pretty much impossible to simultaneously split your brain between work and love. We girls all pretty much live and breathe for passion and romance, for someone to hold our hands, kiss our tears, and make us feel pretty, so how can you possibly do your job to the best of your ability when your head is in the clouds or down the pants of someone you work with?

Look at Monica Lewinski. That girl had the internship of a lifetime, and could have gone on to do anything she wanted with that White House shit on her résumé. If she had been focusing on her career instead of interesting new places to put cigars, maybe she would have beaten Hillary to be our first female candidate. (Isn't that ironic?) Instead, she will basically be doing the walk of shame every morning for the rest of her life. Be smart, girls. You are a Hot Chick, but you are more than just a pretty plaything, so don't let the attention of some man fuck you up♥ at work. Keep your eye on the prize instead of a penis and you are sure to get much further in life than straddled on some fax machine with your skirt around your knees and your integrity even lower.

We want you to find the love that you deserve so much that we wrote a whole book on it—but not when you're on the clock. Your job was designed to supply you with a paycheck and hopefully health insurance, not the man of your dreams! Your job is your job and not your personal dating service, so focus on doing your job well and efficiently so that you have time after hours to go out and find a perfect relationship somewhere else.

# Rules for Workplace Romance

Don't worry; we're not going to leave you hanging. We don't want you to look for love at work, but we're not totally naïve; we know that it might happen no matter what we say. Mixing work and love is like playing with illegal fireworks—it might blow up in your face and destroy your entire career, but if you follow our romance rules for business booty, the only pink slips in your life will be in your lingerie drawer.

## Romance Rule #1: Don't Mix Alcohol with Colleagues

Well, duh, if you go out for martinis every Friday with the three hot guys in accounting, of course you're going to end up going home with at least one of them! Have some self-control and self-respect like the Hot Chick that you are, and don't risk putting yourself in a situation where you're going to end up doing something that you'll only remember when you watch it the next day on YouTube.

## Romance Rule #2: Make Sure It's Worth It

What makes it worth it, you ask? Well, what would you be willing to lose your job over? What would make it worth it for you to stand in the unemployment line, go on endless interviews, and eat ramen noodles for three meals a day? If you consider the passion, chemistry, and possibly love between you and this guy you work with to be worth possibly losing your job and sanity for, then go for it. However, neither a quickie with the office lothario who's worked his way through your entire department nor a sloppy make out session with the bartender at your restaurant's holiday party are worth losing your job, your reputation, or your self-respect over. Listen to your instincts and make sure you won't end up bashing your head into the wall of your office in regret over other things you did against that wall.

## Romance Rule #3: No Married Men No Matter What

It's completely stupid to sleep with a married man under any circumstances, but sleeping with a married man you work with is asking for way more trouble than you can possibly be prepared for. We don't care how much that hot married man you work with says that his wife won't put out, treats him like shit, and just lives for the kids, or that he's leaving her and he actually loves you; you are not allowed to mess with him until, if, and when he and his wife are actually divorced and one of you has another job. If all of those things happen and you still want to be together, go for it—but no nookie whatsoever until then. Whether you're at work or not, fooling around with another woman's man tells the universe♥ that you are too lame and LSE♥ to ever deserve a relationship of your own. Plus, when other people at work find out that you're sleeping with a married man (because they always do), you'll instantly lose the respect of your boss and your colleagues and spark the fury of every married lady in your entire office. Everyone will know that you are a sleazy home wrecker who should never be trusted, admired, or taken seriously. Don't believe that all the good ones are taken, and remember that if he's hitting on you and he's taken, then he's not a good one, anyway!

## Romance Rule #4: Get a Life

One great way to prevent yourself from becoming romantically involved with the people you work with is to create a fantastic social life for yourself outside of work. Once again, it's all about balance, ladies. Sure, you might meet the man of your dreams on the job, but you can't (and shouldn't) count on that. In fact, you should make every effort not to. If you work eighty hours a week and only ever see daylight from your tiny office window, of course you're going to end up hooking up with men you work with. Start living your heyday♥ to the fullest outside of work and this will be less likely to happen. We know that you have to work hard, but you can still throw a party on Saturday night or online date from your very own workplace (only during lunch breaks, please). Make sure that you aren't living at work and you'll be a lot less likely to find romance where you're looking for a promotion.

**Romance Rule #5: Stay off the Office Furniture**
Okay, fine, you met someone at work, the connection is real, and you two just can't help but rip each other's clothes off because you're so damn twitterpated♥. Go ahead and rip each other's clothes off all you want, but don't do it at work! Even if you're doing it with a colleague, you have to keep the booty away from the business. Workplace romances should never actually take place at the workplace, no matter how tempting it may be to surprise him in the morning by chaining yourself to his desk wearing nothing but his tie. If the thrill of doing it at work won't stop calling your names, go to work when you are absolutely sure that nobody will be there (even the cleaning crew), lock the door to your office, and do it on your desk just once to get it out of your nasty system. (Or if you work in a restaurant, keep the door propped open in the meat locker and make sure to wash your hands when you're done.) Do not, however, make a habit of doing it on your desk or in the parking garage, broom closet, break room, or your boss's office! Work when you're at work and save getting off for when you actually get off, and everything in your life will go much more smoothly.

## Romance Rule #6: Don't Give Head to Get Ahead

Don't you dare for one moment think that being a Hot Chick means using your beauty or boobs to sleep your way to the top. Why would you want to tell your boss and the universe♥ that you are nothing but an object whose sexuality can be bought and sold like, um, a prostitute? Sorry if that sounds harsh, but if you are having sex with someone in order to get a raise or a promotion, you are in effect having sex for money, which technically makes you a whore. Have we still not convinced you? Then think about the fact that you will actually be more successful if you keep your panties in their place instead of trying to sleep your way up the corporate ladder. The CEO is not going to trust you to be in charge once he's seen your nipple ring. Offering sexual favors in exchange for a promotion is basically an invitation for the powers that be to disrespect, use, and then fire your hot ass before your boss's handprint is even off of it. Save the slurping for your happy hour margarita and you'll be glad that you did.

## Romance Rule #7: Check Your Feelings at the Door

If you do get romantically involved at work, you need to be mature about it and set up some ground rules with this fine young man of yours. The first rule you two should make is to deal with all relationship-related arguments, emotions, and issues out of the office and long after business hours are over. The last thing you need is for your colleagues to overhear the two of you fighting in the coffee room about the dirty dishes at home or for the two of you to snip at each other across the conference table at meetings because of a fight you had the night before. Likewise, don't get all swoony-eyed at the office and enthusiastically agree with every boneheaded idea he comes up with at a brainstorming meeting just because they come out of his pretty mouth. Try to stay objective and retain your credibility by supporting him on things you actually agree with and politely speaking up against those you don't. While you're at it, expect the same from him. Don't break down crying at a business conference because he went with someone else's suggestion or pick a fight with him after work because his idea was chosen over yours. Keep your business and your relationship as separate as possible, and both of them will feel a lot less like work.

**Romance Rule #8: Freelance Feelings**
If you meet someone at a temporary job, please hold off on getting involved with him until your contract is up. You know you can wait two months to jump in the sack with this guy, and it will totally be worth it not to be remembered as the girl who worked there for a third of the year and slept with two-thirds of the company. This is especially important for you freelance girls, because you will most likely need to go back to this business for a reference, and you want them to be able to speak positively about something more relevant than your blowjob skills. If you work from home, you also need to be diligent about keeping your work and personal lives apart. We know how hard it is in these cases to figure out when the work day starts and ends and when it's time to stop working and start screwing or even eat dinner, so set balanced business hours and each of these activities will be much more pleasurable.

**Romance Rule #9: Deny, Deny, and then Deny Some More**
Honestly, if you're sleeping with someone you work with, everyone is going to find out no matter what you do. We're not totally sure how this happens, but trust us that it does. Your colleagues will be able to smell the interoffice sex on you like too much Axe Effect. However, we think that unless you are engaged, living together, or

actually married, you should deny that any funny business is going on between you. This way, if it simply doesn't last or ends in disaster, you can pretend that nothing happened instead of having to explain to everyone at work that he cheated on you with your roommate, or that you couldn't deal with his strange foot fetish anymore. Talk to your girlfriends outside of work about his cute little quirks and annoying habits, but don't rub your relationship in your coworkers' faces or they might start to resent, distrust, and question you. The office is going to gossip and guess, but why add fuel to the fire when you're already playing with one?

### Romance Rule #10: Act Like a Hot Chick

Do we need to remind you that you are a confident, empowered Hot Chick who can have any man she wants and should never give her power away to any man, especially one she works with? If you slipped up and went home with that irresistible coworker after happy hour, don't you dare feel LSE♥ when you walk past his desk the next day or spend one nanosecond worrying about why he hasn't called! Call him (after work) and say, "Sorry, Jack—that was a mistake. Can we please pretend that nothing happened?" You'll both be relieved to get it out in the open. Acting like a Hot Chick at work also means not saying flirty shit just to get attention from the boys. No bragging about your multi-orgasmic status in the elevator, telling the guys in the cafeteria how much you hate it when guys get jizz in your hair, or running down the hotel hallway drunk and topless on a business trip.

# Chemistry with Colleagues

## A Common Crisis

We've already addressed what you should do if you're single and you find yourself having undeniable, magical♥, crazy-ass chemistry with someone at work, but it can often get even more complicated that that. You might be in a relationship or he might be taken when you find yourself in this situation, and you may be forced to work with someone every day that you have all of these feelings for and not be able to act on them. You might be partnered on a project or have to take a business trip together, and all the sexual tension burning between the two of you might make working together next to impossible. This might really piss off our husbands (sorry!), but we are all human and made up of the same electrical, magical♥ stuff that makes us laugh, cry, feel, and love. Even getting married doesn't change this or deaden our senses, and at some point we're all going to experience colleague chemistry. You just need to be prepared and know how to deal with it.

Even if you have the best job on the planet, you probably spend more time at work than at home with your lover. By the time we fight rush hour and get home to our men, we have about one good hour to scarf down dinner together before we fall asleep on the couch. Then, in your most awake hours—when you're on your game, exuding all of your Hot Chick goodness on the job—it's tough not to feel things for that cool guy at work. You'll notice that as you start acting like a Hot Chick more and more on the job, chemistry with colleagues will become an even bigger problem. You're acting confident, savvy, passionate, and honest; of course men are going to be drawn to you! That's why it's so important that you check yourself when it feels like the universe ♥ is pushing you towards someone in the office.

If a man you work with tells you that he wants you or actually makes a move, you have to be brutally honest and cut it off before it goes any further. Tell him, "I agree that there is an attraction between us, but we can't act on it." Tell him that it would have been fun in another lifetime, but you are in love with your boyfriend and are not going to risk ruining your relationship. Or if you're single and he's the taken one, say, "I respect Susie too much to get involved with you." Try to turn the connection between you into an honest friendship that won't destroy your home or work life. Actively fight off the chemistry with the same amount of power that's pulling you towards each other and it will be much easier to get where you want to be in your career and in your heart.

On the other hand, if he's not saying anything and you're the one with a desperate crush at work, you need to keep your mouth shut. It may seem like the grass is greener at his house, but it's not. That grass actually has just as many potholes, wasps' nests, and piles of dog shit as your yard at home. It's just waiting there for you to uncover it! Remember that he would never reveal his neuroses and hang-ups at work, so right now you're only seeing him in his best light. Trading your man in for a colleague you have good flirty banter with will not solve all of the problems in your current relationship. You'll only be swapping one set of issues for another.

If you're realistic and expect this to happen, it will be a lot easier to handle. We know people who've been caught off guard by chemistry at work. They mistook it for love when it was nothing more than a harmless spark, and messing with that flicker caused it to detonate in their faces. Acknowledge to yourself that chemistry happens to the best of us and remember that it's natural and harmless, but don't douse the flame with gasoline by indulging in enticing emails with someone you have chemistry with, or by going out for drinks with him alone. You're only putting yourself in harm's way by encouraging harmless chemistry to become something much more destructive. After countless cozy happy hours and shared lunches, will anyone be surprised when you turn to this other guy in a weak moment and end up damaging both of your lives? Make an effort to keep your panties on, your head in your work, and your heart at home; it will be well worth it.

# Chapter 8

## *Interoffice Interactions*

WITH ALL OF THE GOSSIP, DRAMA, AND CATTINESS, WORK CAN OFTEN FEEL LIKE A TRASHY REALITY SHOW WITH A GIANT CLUSTER FUCK OF PERSONALITIES THAT YOU HAVE TO NAVIGATE IN ORDER TO SURVIVE. It's not easy, but how you deal with your bitchy boss, handle a nasty nemesis, or plot a course through office gossip can determine how pleasant or miserable your work life is. The emotional shit that coworkers and superiors drag you through can be just as debilitating and hurtful as arguments with your boyfriend about money or fights with your mother about wedding locations.

Well, you have to deal with these people every day and we don't want irritating interoffice interactions to keep you from working and living like a Hot Chick, so get ready for a giant ass kicking, some lovely validation, and a lot of solid information about how to deal with all the crap at work that is not in your job description. Remember, all you gals who work in video stores or as parking attendants can take the word "interoffice" figuratively, because we know that you have to handle the same bullshit as the rest of us. Now let us help you avoid stepping in it!

# Colleague Conundrums

We like to blame clashing personalities at work on conflicting astrological signs (because it's fun), but this can actually be a giant problem that will really ruin your working life if you're not careful. And when your work life is destroyed, the rest of your life can get screwed up, too, because everything in life is connected like in that frustrating game, Jenga. Never underestimate the power of fucked up♥ coworkers. Those bitches (or assholes; we don't discriminate) can plot against you until you're so LSE♥ that they've completely taken over your power. But have no fear; we've been though just about every possible crappy colleague conundrum, and our experience is going to teach you how to handle every annoying coworker like the Hot Chick that you are so that the next time a bullish Taurus or crabby Cancer reads your emails over your shoulder, makes a passive-aggressive comment about your lunch, or simply says, "You look really tired," you'll be able to let it roll off your shoulders like one of those flowing water signs.

## Ten Types of Crappy Colleagues (and How to Deal with Them)

### Callously Competitive

*Description:* This is the girl who is on a mission to one up you every single time. If you get a compliment from your boss, she will do something dramatic just to get a bigger accolade. If you're working together on a project, she will manipulate things so that she can take credit for the entire success of the assignment. She comes in early and stays late just to look good, but she spends hours at her desk itemizing her taxes and wasting time. Then she makes nasty comments behind your back when you have to leave twenty minutes early to go to the doctor. Her competition with you may not be strictly work related. She'll compare boyfriends, boob size, and even the size of your respective engagement rings! It seems like this girl's only goal in life is to beat you at everything, and it's making you absolutely crazy.

*Colleague Counsel:* Well, this girl automatically isn't a Hot Chick because Hot Chicks never compete against other women, especially at work. The worst part about working with this girl is that she can start to make you go against your Hot Chick nature and become paranoid and a little bit competitive. It's hard not to obsess about what she's doing, who she's talking about, and what her next move may be, but if you do this you are letting the terrorists win! She is trying to get you off your game so she can swoop in and trample you, and the more time you spend worrying about her, the less focused you will be on your job, your success, and your own life! We know it's hard, but you have to ignore this bitch and let your hatred for her fire you up to move ahead in your own career. Go ahead and compete, but not with her! Always be genuine, honest, and try to one up *yourself,* and pretty soon she will be eating your dust.

**Perpetual PMS Princess**
*Description:* This is the girl who is always having some sort of crisis. She has a weekly meltdown about trivial things like the inadequacies of the post office and throws a giant tantrum every time she has to deal with a customer service representative. Or maybe she *is* the customer service representative and treats her clients worse than Kate treated poor Jon. This bipolar bitch cries at least once a week and comes to work with a foonge face ♥ pretty much every day. She always has something to complain about, like her back pain, her evil stepfather, or the fact that she doesn't have a doorman, and she often lets her personal life interfere with her job.

*Colleague Counsel:* No matter how nice you are to this girl or how many times you suggest things like counseling, yoga, and Prozac, she won't listen because she loves living with drama. She'll just find some reason to complain about how yoga is too stressful because she has bad memories of being hit on by a lecherous lesbian instructor. Here's a secret, though: girls like this thrive on drama, and if they don't get their fix, they melt quicker than the Wicked Witch of the West. Simply stop giving her your ear and sympathy. Her outbursts will increase at first, but then they'll start dying off like cockroaches after bingeing on Raid pellets. If that doesn't work, try being honest: sit her down and explain that she needs to keep her personal life personal. Hopefully she will be so embarrassed by the knowledge that her childish, unprofessional behavior is affecting other people that she'll be scared silent.

## Creepy Copycat

*Description:* This is the girl who asks where you cut your hair and then shows up on Monday with an identical haircut and dye job. She buys the same bag and laptop as you, and then finds herself a boyfriend who she says is "so much like your boyfriend, it's scary." She orders exactly what you do for lunch pretty much every day. You might think that this crazy-ass *Single White Female* shit only happens in movies, but it has happened to us on more than one occasion and it is super creepy, not to mention a huge distraction at work. You are a Hot Chick and there are girls out there who want to be like you (or might actually want to *be* you)—and they can make your workdays a living nightmare.

*Colleague Counsel:* You may have previously been work buddies with this girl, but you need to cut her out of your life. Just turn a cold shoulder and let her know that you're not going to be the two peas in the same pod that she's envisioning. You have to work with her, so continue to be polite and courteous, but stop there.

Don't start competing with her or making nasty comments about her to your other colleagues. That will only make *you* seem like the competitive one. Just try your hardest to ignore her behavior and never leave her alone with your husband or let her know where you live. If it keeps getting worse, get a restraining order so you don't end up with a stiletto anywhere but on your sexy little feet.

### Condescending C U Next Tuesday

*Description:* She is the queen of the backhanded compliment and constantly says things like, "Wow, you look nice, how early did you have to get up to look like that?" She will also make condescending remarks about how you do your job and try to make you feel stupid if you haven't heard the latest bit of gossip. She will take any speck of weakness you show and use it to make you feel stupid, pathetic, and lame.

*Colleague Counsel:* You may not realize it, but this chick is so insanely jealous of you that she doesn't know what to do with herself. That's why she's putting you down, so that she can try to make herself feel better. It might be hard, but you have to call her on her bullshit behavior. Tell her flat out that you don't appreciate her backhanded compliments or her sassy remarks. Be prepared for her to turn it on you and say, "I didn't mean it that way, you're being way too sensitive, yadda, yadda, yadda. . . . " Ignore that crap and notice how she suddenly stops shoving shit sandwiches down your throat once she knows that you don't have a taste for them.

### Lazy Lollygagger

*Description:* She procrastinates with every assignment and you often have to do her job for her because she's so damn busy dragging her feet. This girl may do everything slowly and seem perpetually stoned or she might have the uncanny ability to find a cute black dress on a thirty-minute lunch break but is just super lazy about her job. Her lackadaisical attitude has a huge (negative) impact on how you do your job because you're always covering for her, and that makes you want to slap her across the face just to get her going.

*Colleague Counsel:* First, you have to stop covering for her. You're just enabling this crap by never forcing her to deal with the consequences. If you're working on something together, say, "I need you to finish this today or it's going to make both of us look bad," and if she still doesn't do it, simply say to your boss, "I'm still waiting for Betty's portion so I can wrap this up." If you wait tables with her and she's used to you covering her section because she can't handle the pressure, just stop doing it. Some customers may suffer, but eventually your boss will notice that she's the slacker and scream at her like Gordon Ramsay, and that will really be satisfying. If you're up front and honest with everyone and stand your ground, you'll be a lot less likely to be blamed for her laziness in the long run.

### Super Snooper

*Description:* This chick cannot keep her big-ass nose out of your ass or your business. She acts like work is a game of twenty questions about your life, reads emails over your shoulder, listens to your phone conversations, and then asks follow-up questions as if she was meant to hear every word. As if that's not bad enough, she may also go through your desk and your emails when you're not at work and has been known to grab your cell phone or camera and start looking through pictures like she's your best fucking friend! The confusing part is that this girl is usually really sweet and seemingly harmless. She's just bored with her own life and can't help but be fascinated by your amazing Hot Chick self, but her snooping behavior is as out of control as a really unfortunate case of Tourette's.

*Colleague Counsel:* She's like a begging puppy, and you need to stop feeding her with bits of information if you want her to learn her lesson. Don't have private conversations in her presence, turn the computer off when you leave your desk, and never keep personal documents at work. Think about it—if you give your dog some steak off your plate every time he begs, he'll just keep doing it, but if you firmly say no, he'll whimper and walk way with his tail between his legs and learn to nourish himself with his own dog food. We're very sorry to say it, but you have to treat this bitch like a dog and teach her to entertain herself with her own life.

## Mean Monster

*Description:* This woman is quite different from the condescending one because she doesn't even try to mask her nastiness with fake roses and sunshine. She is just plain old mean, malicious, and hateful. She screams, yells, uses profanity, and does not hesitate to rip you a brand new asshole right in front of everyone you work with. Ouch.

*Colleague Counsel:* The hard part is that colleagues usually don't have the balls to treat you like this, so it's often your superiors who are the mean-ass monsters. Being in a negative environment like this can really take a toll on your psyche and can prevent you from working like a Hot Chick because you're so scared that you're going to get either your head bitten off or your ass chewed out. There is no excuse for cruel, volatile behavior like this, so either discreetly talk to HR about the situation, start looking for a new job, or both. Whatever you do, work extra hard not to let her mean spirit ruin your mojo. Focus on yourself and how you're going to get away from this monster, vent to your friends after work, and try not to let her hold you back.

### Ditzy Dingbat

*Description:* It's very frustrating to have to work with people who are as dumb as a proverbial doornail. This chick is either actually stupid and says things like, "Of course I've never read the Bible because I'm not that religious," or she is technically book smart but has a disconnected thought process that is impossible to follow and causes her to include five thousand mistakes in everything she does. We often wonder how this girl got hired in the first place. Did she give good interview, or give something else good during the interview?

*Colleague Counsel:* You probably can't improve this girl's IQ or stop her from saying the dumbest things on the planet, but you can improve your working environment by kindly taking a bit of control. Without being condescending, tell her that her lack of attention to her work is making your job a lot harder. Ask her if there's anything you can do to help her focus. Hopefully she'll feel as dumb as she is and at least *try* to do a better job. Remember to be kind, though, because she doesn't mean to be ditzy; it's just who she is. (Unless, of course, you think that she's playing dumb to get out of doing work or to get attention, in which case you should slap that bitch across the face right now.)

### Braggy Bitch

*Description:* This woman thinks that your whole company (and possibly the entire universe♥) might just dissolve without her fabulous presence, and she finds a way to brag about every single mundane thing that she does. She can come in two forms: the beautiful, intelligent, accomplished woman who is just endlessly pleased with herself, and the far less impressive woman who over-compensates by constantly tooting her own horn. Either type can provoke serious fantasy sequences♥ about this bitch getting fired or (better yet) falling down a steep flight of stairs.

*Colleague Counsel:* It may seem like you're the only one who sees her true colors, but trust us; they are just as visible (and obnoxious) as your slutty Rainbow Brite Halloween costume. Everyone is just humoring her by acting impressed by her various bullshit accomplishments, so don't feel the need to point out her weaknesses or compete by bragging about yourself, too. Remember that she is not acting like a Hot Chick, but you can act like one by simply ignoring her and going about your business. Before long, everyone will be singing your praises so loudly that they'll finally drown her out.

### Fake Floozy

*Description:* She is a giant phony liar who can't be trusted with anything, whether it's a corporate credit card or your husband. She'll find a way to skim money off the top, to fudge her petty cash receipts, and expense trips to the spa. While she's at it, she'll take credit for everyone else's work and try to steal your man. She is, quite clearly, the worst!

*Colleague Counsel:* At the risk of stating the obvious, don't ever give this girl an opportunity to take advantage of you. Don't tell her anything that you don't want broadcast to the entire company, like the fact that you slept with the UPS guy or that you have a tattoo of the Incredible Hulk's signature on your inner thigh. If you're this woman's superior, make her first on your list of layoffs because she should be punished for taking advantage of the system. If you're equals and she's really doing something destructive, then you should tell your boss. If you know about her thievery and don't tell, you could be implicated one day—plus bosses always reward employees who are looking out for the company's best interest.

**Are You a Crappy Colleague?!**

It's fun to label your coworkers as the different types of crappy colleagues, but if you recognize yourself in any of these examples, you need to cut that shit out right now. You'll never find true happiness or have a magical♥ heyday♥ if you don't live up to your full potential at work. Even if you truly hate your job, despise your coworkers, and loathe your boss, you should not act condescending, untrustworthy, lazy, mean, or dumb at work. You should be acting like the confident Hot Chick that you are at all times, and especially on the job. Stop acting overly competitive, snooping, or trying to be just like the tall, skinny blonde you work with and focus on being a better you! You are a Hot Chick and you have so much fabulous goodness inside of you, so take this opportunity to squash any LSE♥ and start acting like the confident, savvy girl that we know you can be.

# Nasty Nemeses

We keep telling you not to compete with other women at work and we stand by that, but we know that there is one girl you work with who just makes your skin crawl—and the truth is that she can't stand you, either. Like it or not, you may have found yourself with an office nemesis. Having a nemesis is actually quite common, and most women other than Mother Teresa have one. LC has Heidi, Jennifer Aniston has Angelina Jolie, and Rosie has Elizabeth Hasselbeck (not to mention Donald Trump and Kelly Ripa). You don't even have to work in an office to have an office nemesis, but you do need to take control of the situation before it spins into a crazy catfight worthy of the tabloids.

We've had our share of nemeses—one who left us nasty notes on our car and another who always "accidentally" left us off of every important company-wide email—and the most helpful thing we did to make the best of the situation was to act like Hot Chicks and not compete. We knew that we were cooler than those bitches, and so are you—so the best way to handle your nemesis is to laugh and gossip about it *outside* of the workplace and treat her with complete respect in the office. Call your girl-friends after work (boyfriends usually aren't any good at this type of thing) and make fun of her awful, nasally voice. Pretty soon your hatred will turn into laughter and she'll be no more menacing than a fun party joke.

Then while you're at work, cut the shit talking and the back-stabbing and say things like, "Oh, I'm sure she means well. . . ." This might piss her off even more, but it will be her problem, not yours. Always remember that you are a Hot Chick and you have no excuse to ever be cruel or catty. Act with class and try to empathize; there is probably a deep-rooted reason why she sucks so badly. Maybe she was cheated on by eight men, ripped off by Bernie Madoff, or something even worse. Try attacking her with all of your Hot Chick charm and see if you can't win even her over. We bet you can.

# Gossip Girls

When it's two a.m. and you and your girlfriends are drinking champagne and painting your toenails, it's okay to vent about how you can't stand that nosy bitch you work with, but gossiping on the job can be as dangerous as casually sleeping with your best friend's man. It might be fun and thrilling for a minute, but if someone overhears or the source of your goss session finds out about it, you'll end up hurting another Hot Chick and simultaneously destroying your own reputation. Oh, and just in case you were wondering, salary level is not equally proportional to gossip authority. If you're the boss, gossiping about your underlings will make them resent you even more, which certainly isn't a good way to motivate your troops. It doesn't matter if you're a big shot corporate lawyer or paying your way through art school by working at Auntie Anne's; gossip can always lead to trouble.

Of course, we know that there are tame, harmless forms of gossip. It's possible that you're spreading nice rumors, like how excited you are for your coworker's surprise baby shower or her promotion. That's fine, but it doesn't really count as gossip. We're defining gossip as anything scandalous or inherently negative, like debating whether the IT guy is wearing a toupee or if the slutty receptionist even *owns* a bra. Since gossip is associated with hatred, complaints, and pessimism, it is also a form of passion. You don't have to love someone to be passionate about them; hate is passion, too, and oftentimes is even more powerful. Think about your obsession with the way your coworker eats her lunch, or her bizarre wardrobe choices. That is passion you are feeling for those girls, passion and energy that you could be using for something positive, instead—like figuring out what you want in life, having a magical♥ heyday♥, or getting ahead at work.

We know that you can't stand the very sight of some people at your job (or maybe it's just that you can't stand your actual job); maybe you've just decided that everyone there is a stupid waste of space. Maybe it's because you have to share a tiny workspace with them, are forced to travel to lame business conferences with them, or perhaps it's simply because they're associated with the job that you hate. Either way, the best way for you to get ahead and be happy at work is to stop being a hater. Quit complaining and gossiping about your coworkers and use that excitement and power to move your career forward and get excited about your life, instead. Put all of that vigor into yourself instead of other people. You can use it in your career or even another aspect of your life, like your relationship with your boyfriend or your daily yoga class. Whatever you do, quit giving away your passion to people who annoy you and keep it for your savvy Hot Chick self, instead!

# Gossip Alert

In case we haven't convinced you yet, here are ten good reasons not to gossip at work. Consider yourself warned.

### 1—Energy Suck
The energy you're putting into hating your colleagues and talking shit about them at work is the same energy that you could be using to actually do your job. Ignore that bitch and her strange makeup techniques and put that fire into your career, instead.

### 2—Time Waster
Don't you wish you had a few more hours in the day to do your job, run errands, and maybe even squeeze in some fun? Well, why don't you start by saving yourself five hours a week just by shutting your mouth? The minutes you spend flapping your jaws is taking precious time away from your own life.

### 3—Karma Counts
You can be sure that if you are gossiping about someone else, another girl is gossiping about you. It's about as certain as gravity, death, and taxes (and almost as miserable as all three). When you gossip, people lose respect for you, resent you, and therefore consider you a perfect target for their own gossip match.

### 4—It Mirrors You
You may think the weird, way too tan girl you're gossiping about is a total loser, but when you talk a lot of smack, it actually turns *you* into a negative, bitchy loser—and it doesn't take long for other people to notice. Swallow that nasty gossip like a giant fish oil pill

and let people see the real you—a Hot Chick who is smart enough to keep her mouth shut.

### 5—It's Mean

We're not a couple of Goody-Two-Shoes or anything, but gossiping is fucked up ♥. You don't know what people are going through, why that girl is really always late to work, or why she's turning orange from eating a bag of baby carrots for lunch every day. Wouldn't you feel awful if you found out she had a serious illness or something? Stop being so cruel and you won't risk making a huge ass out of yourself.

### 6—They're There

You have to work with these people, ladies! It's fine if they're not your favorite people on the planet, but gossiping about them will only make you hate them more, which will in turn make it even more difficult to work with them. The more you complain about someone, the more they get under your skin, so make a conscious effort to keep your mouth shut and eventually they won't bug you quite so much!

### 7—The Universe ♥ Listens

As cheesy as this may sound, the universe ♥ pays attention to where you are putting your energy, so the longer you spend your days cracking jokes about your boss's sweat stains or acting jealous of your coworker's seemingly perfect life, the more attention the universe ♥ will pay to those people instead of you. Help yourself get some love from the world by focusing on your own actions, and pretty soon you'll be the one with the perfect life that others envy (hopefully sans the sweat stains).

### 8—The Golden Rule ♥

It was true when you were three and didn't want to share your toys with your brother, and it's true at work now. Imagine it was you those girls were gossiping about. Wouldn't it make you feel totally LSE♥ to know that people were spending all day hating on you? Then why are you participating instead of treating your coworkers with the same respect you want them to treat you with? Find something else to do with your mouth (not *that*, you're at work!) and you'll be glad that you did.

### 9—It Brings You Down

Tomorrow, when someone asks you how you are, just try saying, "Great" instead of launching into a full-blown complaint monologue about the girl in your carpool. You'll be amazed at how good it feels not to be dragged down into the depths of depression by your own complaints and nasty chitchat. Comment on the fact that Jane has nice eyes instead of saying that she looks eight months pregnant and you'll be all the happier for it.

### 10—It Makes You Look Bad

Do you want a promotion, a raise, better hours, or weekends off? Well, have you ever heard of the term "team player," or noticed that it's in pretty much every job description on the planet? Bosses (like third-grade teachers) appreciate people who play well with others and don't waste their time cutting each other down. Stop doing yourself a disservice by making yourself look like a catty slacker instead of a promotable Hot Chick!

# Get in on Gossip and Get out Unscathed

Sometimes gossiping can be part of your job. You may have to engage in conversations with people about other people in order to socialize at work and make people like you, and you can totally do this as long as you're always kind and respectful. If you turn up your nose at every gossip session and give your colleagues a lecture like the one we just gave you, that won't make you very likeable, either. The trick is to find the compromise between being communal and being a conspirator, and if you follow our rules, you'll be able to partake in chitchat without it coming back to bite you in your hot little ass. It's as easy as 1, 2, 3. . . .

### 1—Nod, Smile, Giggle, and Haul Ass

If you're lunching with one of your superiors and he tells you that a woman you work with slept with the entire company soccer team, you may need to make him feel like it was okay for him to tell you that. Just nod, smile, act surprised, make a joke, and then excuse yourself to the ladies' room. The more you can just *act* like you are participating without actually saying a single incriminating word that he can repeat at his next lunch, the more you will appear to be gracious and kind, but still the kind of girl who's fun to be around and easy to talk to.

### 2—Use Your Friends

If a girl you work with invites everyone at your company to her birthday party except you or says to you at lunch, "I'm glad you're here because all the other girls we work with are so skinny," you might be tempted to pull five coworkers into the supply closet and start tearing her to shreds with every nasty word you can come up with. But if you do this it will really only make you look jealous and insecure. Hold your tongue and call a girlfriend you don't work with and vent to her, instead. Your friends can sympathize (we've all been there), will certainly side with you, and complaining to them instead of getting revenge at work will keep you from looking nasty and LSE♥.

**3—Turn Cattiness into Compassion**
The best way to always be seen in a positive light is to decide to act with respect and compassion towards the people that bother you instead of always being mean. This will also help you respect yourself and see a Hot Chick in the mirror rather than a vile, conniving rumormonger. The next time you're at a work-related happy hour and everyone else starts tearing one of your colleagues apart, stand up for her without getting all haughty about it. Say something like, "Come on, guys, if your husband left you with three kids and a huge mortgage to run away to Bali with an eighteen-year-old stewardess, you might be kind of moody, too." Reminding everybody of how hateful and ugly they're acting without actually saying, "You guys are acting hateful and ugly" will shut them up and make them respect you, and you'll all be able to move on to the happy part of happy hour.

# Win over Your Boss without Kissing Ass

It's nearly impossible to work like a Hot Chick if you don't get along with your boss, and that negative relationship can send disturbing shock waves throughout the rest of your life faster than the ones Michael Jackson's death sent around the globe. Even if you and your boss have a decent relationship, it can be difficult to know how to act around her. Do you kiss up to him and laugh at all his stupid jokes, or treat her like your mom or one of your friends? We know what it's like to feel totally LSE♥ around a superior and not know what to say, how to act, or how far, deep, and wide the butt smooching should go. After surviving many different jobs (and bosses), we've figured out how to handle this relationship delicately without letting it get the best of us, and we want to pass this knowledge on to you. Once you know how to maintain a healthy relationship with your boss, your entire life will feel so much more balanced and beautiful. Check out our techniques for acting like a Hot Chick around your boss, and before you know it your boss will be trying to get in a few kisses on *your* ass!

### 1—Squash LSE♥ Like a Giant Spider

We understand why you might be *feeling* LSE♥, but we certainly hope you're not acting LSE♥ around your superior. The last thing you should show your boss is that you're a weak, insecure pansy ass! She has to trust you, and no matter if you're a flight attendant, a news anchor, or a backup dancer, you want your boss to think that you are strong, capable, and reliable. It's okay to fake it at first—remember that confidence is the only thing a Hot Chick is allowed to fake—because acting LSE♥ can make you feel even more LSE♥ and create a vicious cycle. Act confident, instead, and soon you'll feel that way even if you run into your boss in the restroom (isn't that the worst?)!

## 2—Be Yourself

Stop hiding your true persona around the one person you most want to impress! Don't feel like you have to shy away from your charming self when face-to-face with a superior. Acting natural is a sign of confidence. A good rule is to behave around your boss the same way you would around, say, your mother's best friend. That means you can make appropriate jokes and talk about what you do outside of work, but keep it to yourself if you love dropping f-bombs or moonlight as a "furry." (Have you seen that *Real Sex* episode? We're not judging, but holy shit!) Show your boss all the goodness, intelligence, and savvy that you have, but keep your skeletons at home in your closet. Oh, and we know that it's hard sometimes to know who "yourself" actually is, so if you don't quite know yet, then reread our definition of Hot Chick and be that!

## 3—Stand Up For Yourself

Some bosses really will try to take advantage of you, and it can be very hard to say no to the person who pays your salary. Your boss might make you do a ton of extra work that's not in your job description, be very mean about not giving you a raise or promotion, or make you run truly demeaning personal errands like walking her dog or picking up her birth control pills. We want you to remember that you are not your boss's slave. Your job is supposed to help you move forward in life, so don't be afraid to ask for what you deserve. Tell him that you have taken on a new level of responsibility and feel that you deserve a raise, or that you don't feel comfortable picking up her dog's poop. Maybe she'll agree with you and say yes, but even if it's a no, she'll know that you're not a doormat and probably gain some respect for you if you show some backbone. Plus, now you know for sure that it's time to start looking for another job.

**4—Turn Fear into Fabulousness**
We don't care how loud he yells, how bitchy and passive-aggressive she can be, or how much they try to embarrass you in front of clients and coworkers; you cannot continue to live in fear of this person and let her steal your power! Quit shaking in your knee-high boots every time he walks into a room and turn all of that weird fearful energy into some fabulous Hot Chick vibes. Give yourself a pep talk before every meeting or interaction. Tell yourself that you are a confident, savvy Hot Chick with absolutely nothing to be afraid of (unless, of course, you're a drug dealer or a prostitute and your boss is actually a sex trafficker with a violent criminal record—but if that's the case, we're pretty sure you're not reading this book right now).

**5—Remember That Her Shit Stinks, Too**
Idolizing your boss is as unhealthy as eating a deep-fried Snickers bar. News flash, ladies—her shit stinks, too. (Actually, we don't know exactly what shit smells like, because we've never, ever done it.) Unless your boss is the real Batman, you should not put him or her on a pedestal. Every time you look at her, remember that this is a regular person with a bunch of shoes piled at the bottom of her closet and she probably doesn't floss every day. Sure, we want you to appreciate your boss, and it's great if you actually look up to her—but there is a fine line between seeing her as your role model and being so in awe of her that you cower and act really weird in her presence. If you treat your boss with respect like any other normal person (because she *is* a normal person), pretty soon you'll have a normal, healthy, working relationship.

# Part III

## How to Play Like a Hot Chick

HAVING FUN IS WHAT LIFE IS REALLY ALL ABOUT, BUT MANY OF US ARE SO BUSY WORKING THAT WE FORGET HOW IMPORTANT LEISURE IS AND FEEL GUILTY ABOUT EVERY MOMENT THAT WE SPEND DOING ANYTHING THAT DOESN'T MOVE OUR CAREERS FORWARD OR HELP TAKE CARE OF OUR FAMILIES. Those things are obviously important, but we want all of you Hot Chicks to let your hair down, kick up your four-inch heels, and start having some fun! It's becoming increasingly hard for women to find time for "play," but that's exactly why we think it's so important. How can you truly enjoy your life and feel like a Hot Chick when you're working your hot little butt off around the clock at a job that makes you crazy, spending your nights and weekends trying to deal with your insurance company through some fucked up ♥ automated phone system, getting new brake pads, and standing in line at the grocery store to buy food that you're only going to feel guilty about eating later? Then there are the real tragedies in life, like sickness and death, war, divorces, and financial collapse. All of this stuff can make life feel useless and hardly worth living.

Well, we've been there, and we've found that the only thing that energizes us on even the toughest days is to take control of our lives, put aside everything else that's going on, and find some time to have fun. It may sound frivolous, but we think that fun is as good for your physical and mental health as all of the herbs and yoga classes on the planet. Who decided that we're meant to work ten-hour days and then run errands all weekend? Rethink those rules and make play, fun, leisure, or whatever the hell you want to call it a priority, because we want you to stop and smell the roses before they're all moldy, brittle, and dried up—and you are, too (yikes!).

We hope that by now you are feeling and working like the Hot Chick that you are, because that's the only way to make room in your life for playtime. It's all connected, ladies. The first step to living like a Hot Chick is to feel good about yourself (LSE♥ girls do not love their lives); the second step is to work in a way that fuels your life instead of sucking the life out of it; and the third step is to embrace every other amazing component of your existence. *That* is a balanced life, and we want you to have one by the end of this book—but that will never happen if you don't make it happen. So in this section, we are going to show you exactly how to play like a Hot Chick and begin to create the joyful lifestyle that you dream about. Let's get started!

# Chapter 9

## *This Is Your Heyday*♥

IN THE GLOSSARY, WE DEFINE YOUR HEYDAY♥ AS
"THE VERY BEST, MOST MAGICAL♥, HOTTEST TIME OF
YOUR LIFE—NO MATTER WHAT AGE BOX YOU CHECK,
OR WHETHER YOU'RE MARRIED OR SINGLE, GAY OR
STRAIGHT." Your heyday♥ begins when you stop having a
pity party and decide that you're hot and worth all the fun in
the world." Since we're writing a whole chapter on your heyday♥,
we want to expand on that definition a little bit and clarify a
few things. A heyday♥ does not mean living irresponsibly, getting
shit-faced every night, showing up to work hung over, having endless one-night stands, or covering your body in Hello Kitty tattoos
that you'll surely regret when you have grandchildren. Instead,
your heyday♥ should be about doing whatever it is that makes you
happy. It's the time to throw caution to the wind and start doing
all of the healthy and positive things that help you jump out of
bed in the morning glowing with excitement.

It's up to you to make that kind of heyday♥ happen for yourself. It's kind of like throwing yourself a party. You throw the type of party and live the kind of heyday♥ that matches your personality and makes you happy. You can make it a Tupperware party, a book club party, or a freaking sex toy party! You can serve yourself pizza and beer, fondue and champagne, or organic spinach and tofu cupcakes. Maybe your heyday♥ won't resemble a party at all. For you, it might mean taking meditation classes at an ashram, or volunteering at the local YMCA.

We don't care what your heyday♥ consists of; we just want you to have one. The most important thing is not to wait until you meet the right guy or have twenty grand in the bank to begin your heyday♥; we want you to start it now! Don't wait any longer to start creating moments in your life that bring you joy and planning events that you will look forward to. It's really easy to lose that youthful zest for life as you become increasingly burdened by responsibilities, and we want to bring it back. We're going to walk you through declaring your heyday♥ right this second so that you can start creating the fun times and great memories that will make your entire life worthwhile.

# The Importance of Your Heyday♥

Many Hot Chicks underestimate the importance of a heyday♥ or believe that having fun is trivial and unimportant. Well, that's bullshit. If you're living your life in a tiny box that's filled to the brim with stress and obligations with no room for fun, we know you're not happy. You may be smiling on the outside, but the lack of fun in your life is probably perpetuating the vicious cycle of body image issues, LSE♥, and the constant fear of not being good enough. We went through this, and we realized one day that at that very moment, we were missing our heyday♥ by complaining about the lack of fun in our lives and only seeing the negative side of things. We declared it our heyday♥ right then and there, and our lives changed overnight. We were suddenly more confident, had better friendships, better work lives, and better love in our lives—all thanks to having a better outlook on life. By adding more fun and excitement to our lives, we actually became less stressed. It may sound counterintuitive, but by filling our lives up even more, we ended up feeling much more balanced.

Every one of you Hot Chicks needs to experience a heyday♥, even all you alpha kitties who get off on having everything structured and perfectly scheduled. You need to pencil in some playtime or we're afraid you'll regret it later, and we really want you Hot Chicks to avoid regret at all costs. If you're still not convinced, here are our top five reasons why declaring your heyday♥ is the most important thing you can do for yourself.

### 1—Fight Boredom, Find Energy

Work is easier and Mondays don't suck so hard when your life is full of other fun things that you can look forward to. Plus, your heyday♥ will keep you on your toes and fill you with more energy than a whole case of Emergen-C. Work and other obligations can be boring and draining, and that monotony can become toxic to your mind and body. However, celebrating your heyday♥ will fill you with a newfound sparkle and prevent you from indulging in self-destructive behaviors like eating tubes of raw cookie dough on the couch every night, stalking your boyfriend's ex on Facebook, or watching *The Real Housewives* of whatever city or state you happen to live in. Trade your boredom and doldrums for energy and excitement, and see how much fuller your entire life becomes.

### 2—Combat Depression

Whether you are clinically depressed or just want to kill yourself every twenty-eight days like we do, a heyday♥ truly can help with every kind of depression. We all feel blue from time to time no matter how much fun we are having in life, but when you decide that you deserve to enjoy all of the fun that life has to offer and you make room in your life (and in your head) for play time, you will naturally pull yourself out of the dumps and into a whole new frame of mind. A heyday♥ is (scientifically speaking) more effective than Prozac on crack, so quit playing small♥ and feeling sorry for yourself and start living a life that is the opposite of depressing.

### 3—Heal OWL Syndrome♥

If your OWL Syndrome♥ is so bad that you spend every night crying out of sheer hopelessness only to wake up with mascara stains all over your pillow (and then the thought of doing laundry ends up making you feel even more hopeless), the best cure is to add more to your life. Don't get mad at us; it's true! The trick is to add in things that are relaxing, rejuvenating, and fun, not a million more obligations that you'll dread. Taking time to indulge in the things you enjoy in life will make things like root canals so much more bearable, so start having a heyday♥ that makes your heart happy and see how much less stressful everyday stressors become.

### 4—Heydays♥ Make You Heydayish♥
It's totally true. Try it.

### 5—Become Magically♥ Magnetic
By merely stating that it's your heyday♥ and beginning to act accordingly, your life will change dramatically. It's totally magic♥, just like how your magic♥ jeans make you look ten pounds lighter or an Oprah brow wax makes you look ten years younger. (We love you, Oprah!) That's because no matter how cheesy it sounds, the universe♥ listens to our thoughts and pays attention to our actions. If you think and act like it's your heyday♥, the universe♥ will treat you like it's your heyday♥ by giving you fun things to do and cool people to meet. But the universe♥ isn't the only one paying attention—just see how other people react to your new attitude. Your energy, your zest, and all of the fun you're having will make you magnetic to guys, bosses, and all the other people who need more fun in *their* lives, too. So declare it your heyday♥ right now (damn it!) and start attracting all of that goodness you deserve.

# Learn Your Lessons

Of course, there are deeper benefits to having a heyday♥, too. When you open yourself up to new and exciting things, you will undoubtedly learn something new and exciting about yourself. Experiencing new things is like exercise for your mind and soul, and just like an intense Pilates class, your heyday♥ will help you discover muscles in your spirit that you never knew you had. Precisely what you learn about yourself during your heyday♥ can vary quite a bit. You may discover that no matter how delicious the cosmos on *Sex and the City* look, the fact is that they're just too sweet for you—or that you prefer going *au naturel* and want to give us a giant finger for making you try that bikini wax. We hope you'll also learn something a bit deeper, like the fact that you want to quit your corporate job to open a bakery or stop partying so much and spend more time volunteering.

If you're stuck in a boring routine that sucks the life out of you, of course you're not inspired to go out and get the things you most want out of life—but if you challenge yourself to try new experiences, you will end up feeling more capable, confident, and empowered. A lot of women fear change and actually resist having a heyday♥ because they're nervous about what they will learn. What if they discover that they're in an unhappy marriage or a dead-end job? Well, would you rather live the rest of your life in ignorant bliss or find out what makes you tick right now so that you can start finding true, honest, blissful bliss? Here are a few of the things that you might learn about yourself during your heyday♥; instead of fearing them, we want you to open your mind to these changes so that you can make the most of this magical♥ time of your life.

### 1—You Want to Move

When you start living your heyday♥, you might realize that you're doing it in the wrong place. Many of us stay in one city or town our entire lives and never venture out into the world, but when we start trying new things, we realize that there is so much more out there that we want to discover—and that we can't possibly do it in our sleepy hometowns. Now, we certainly encourage you to branch out, but you must think this one through before taking action. Don't just wake up one morning and start packing up the car. Make a decision and then begin the process of setting up a new life for yourself somewhere else. Most importantly, open your mind to the possibility of living anywhere—the world is big, life is short, and we want you to make the most out of both.

### 2—Your Relationship Is Toxic

When you become happier and start embracing life, it makes sense that your eyes will be opened to the things that are not working in your life. What is preventing you from truly being happy in all aspects of your life? Sadly, you might realize that your toxic relationship or the lack of passion in your relationship is to blame. If this is you, we hope that you will fight for your love with every muscle in your heart and body—and if it still doesn't work, have the courage to move on. Don't be reckless and think that the grass is going to be greener with some dude you meet on a cruise, but be honest with yourself (and your man) about what is or isn't working and act accordingly. This is your heyday♥, and you deserve a love that lifts you up where you belong (thanks, Joe Cocker).

### 3—You Want a Relationship

Similarly, many Hot Chicks who are working too hard or putting everyone else in their lives first will learn during their heyday♥ that they are sick of always being the bridesmaid and want a love of their own. This is a great lesson to learn, because we believe that you will never find the love that you deserve until you know exactly what you want. If your heyday♥ isn't including enough love, don't freak out or feel sorry for yourself. Just tell the universe♥ that you want a committed, loving relationship, then complete the Build-A-Boyfriend program in *How to Love Like a Hot Chick* and the rest will magically♥ fall into place.

**4—Your Priorities Have Changed**

If you're tired of being underpaid, overworked, and scared to death of having children because you don't know how you'll ever be able to afford childcare, we want you to stop obsessing about what you don't have and focus on the abundance in your life, instead. Relax and enjoy your heyday♥, and see what you learn. You will probably discover a new set of priorities and find a way to get what you want. You might learn that having children is your number one goal and find a way to work from home to care for them, or maybe you'll discover that you want a job that's more challenging or more meaningful or more lucrative. It doesn't matter what the change is. What matters is that as soon as you start having more fun and taking time for yourself, you will discover what is truly important to you, which of course will make you so much closer to getting it.

**5—You Just Need a Change**

Sometimes, when you're stuck in a rut, you don't realize how badly you want things to change—it's only when you shake things up that you realize how crusty and sad your life has become. You might even be unsatisfied in many different areas of your life. Don't freak out! It's okay to just want change in general and not know exactly what that change is going to look like or how to make it happen. The best way to handle this is to sit back, buckle your seatbelt, and enjoy every minute of your heyday♥. You don't have to consciously change anything, because by living your hey-day♥ to the fullest, you *are* changing something. What you and your life will look like when you come out on the other end is anybody's guess, but just let go of all your fears and get excited to find out!

# Ten Ways to Jumpstart Your Heyday♥

Now that you know all of the great things that are going to happen to you during your heyday♥, we want you to get this party started. Having the right mindset is really the best way to start your heyday♥, but sometimes it helps to do a little something special to commemorate this new part of your life. Taking specific action makes a statement to the universe♥ (and to yourself) that your heyday♥ has officially begun. Some of these might sound silly, but sometimes the silliest, most insane actions can actually change your life. Try one (or all) of these and start your heyday♥ off on the right note. Don't hold back! Remember that you deserve to have a little crazy fun in your life no matter how old you are, what job you have, and whether you're married or saving yourself for marriage. This is your life, and it's time to balance out all the bullshit that makes it so hard with some fun heyday♥ moments. Here's how you can get started!

## 1—Go See a Psychic

This is actually how we jumpstarted our own heyday♥! It may sound ridiculous, but sitting down with a complete stranger and hearing his or her thoughts about you and your life can inspire you to bust out of your routine, do something different, and start having more fun. Don't take the predictions too literally, but instead allow these unfiltered thoughts about your destiny to motivate you to start living up to your full potential.

## 2—Have a One-Night Stand

We are so sick of getting shit for this, but in honor of the First Amendment (and because they love to talk about this on the *Today* show), we're going to say it again—jumpstart your heyday♥ by having a one-night stand! In our last book we gave a whole set of one-night stand rules which we won't repeat here, but we will remind you that we mean this more figuratively than literally. If your sex chakra is more closed off than the traffic on a Los Angeles freeway, just try opening your mind to the idea of a one-night stand, and please remember that a one-night stand is not when a guy fails to call you back after you have sex with him. It's when you consciously decide to go out and get yourself some commitment-free lovin'.

## 3—Get a Bikini Wax

This is not only a great confidence booster, but having this naughty little secret hiding underneath your clothes might also make you start itching to have more fun. (Oh, but we hope there's no itching!) Please do not try this at home. Go to a professional, pop a few Advil beforehand, and see how it makes you feel. When you start acting bold, you often become motivated to keep on acting bold, so rip it all off and let your heyday♥ begin!

## 4—Change Your Hair

Dramatically changing your looks (without looking like you went on *Extreme Makeover*) is one of the best ways we can think of to make a fresh start. Chopping off or dying your hair is a statement to yourself and the universe♥ that you are starting a new, fun, carefree chapter in your life. Just like the bikini wax, that shit will grow back whether you like it or not—so why not experiment? Superficial little changes like this can transform the way you see yourself and in turn how other people see you, so try a new look and get a new outlook along with it.

## 5—Throw a Party

We kick off each New Year and birthday with a celebration, so why not jumpstart your heyday♥ by throwing a party, too? This is the perfect excuse to get all of your friends together for a night of fun. We want you to celebrate your life and will give you specific advice for party planning in the next chapter, but remember that when you open your life up to more fun, it usually shows up pretty quickly. Don't be surprised if you end up meeting a cute guy or future best friend at your very own heyday♥ party.

## 6—Say It Out Loud and Write It Down

Sometimes saying what you want out loud, whether it's, "I want a piece of chocolate cake," "I want a new job," or, "I want to start my heyday♥ right now," can solidify your commitment to getting it. We don't care if you're alone in the bathroom or out with all of your girlfriends. Just try saying, "I declare the beginning of my heyday♥ right here and now!" Then take it one step further and write it down. Buy a cute heyday♥ journal and fill the pages with all of the fun new things that you want to experience and you'll be one step closer to doing them.

## 7—Find a Friend

It's a lot less fun to have a bunch of new experiences without anyone to laugh with and gossip to about them. Find a partner in crime who will share your heyday♥. Just like a good workout buddy, she can hold you accountable by not letting you turn down invitations, get LSE♥, or spend your entire weekend reorganizing your closets. Plus, you can do all of this fun stuff (well, except maybe the one-night stands) together!

## 8—Wear Something Racy

Toss out those granny panties (or save them for that yucky time of the month) and invest in a whole new wardrobe of sexy little things. Don't for a minute think that it's not worth it if nobody else is going to see your new outfits. Just knowing that you have a glittery thong or naughty garters hiding under your work clothes will make you feel sexy and sassy, and that is the perfect attitude to start your heyday♥ with! Plus, your new confidence might just inspire you to show your new goodies off to a nice young man, and there's certainly no harm in that.

## 9—Get out of Town

Travelling, whether it's to another country or just another county, is a great way to get a fresh new outlook on life and rediscover all of the goodness that the world has to offer. Seeing how other people live can change your perspective and remind you that life is not all about work and responsibilities. We'll be giving you more travel advice later, but for now, why not start saving up for a trip that will jumpstart your new life in a whole new time zone?

## 10—Move out of Town

Okay, this one is a little dramatic and probably sounds impossible for many of you, but (kind of like the one-night stand thing) we just want you to open your mind to the possibility of it. Are you bored in your hometown or living somewhere that you hate just because of your job? Well, then why not start looking for a job in another city or exploring the world until you find the place that you'd most like to live? Remember, your heyday♥ is all about making the most of this one life, and we want you to live it out in a place that inspires, excites, and nurtures you.

# Magical ♥ Master Plan (MMP)

Now it's time to dig a little further and think about your most secret desires. Many of us limp though our lives wondering what the hell we're doing on this planet in the first place. Is there a purpose to our lives? What are we destined to do, who are we supposed to be, and where the heck is that perfect man who we should be with? We don't want you to wake up one day with your boobs at your knees and realize that you missed out, did it all wrong, and never lived up to your full potential. Instead, we want you to live your life to its absolute fullest so that your only regret is that this book wasn't published sooner!

Some people believe that you only learn important life lessons through the hardships and heartaches that make you stronger, but we don't want you to sit around waiting for the shit to hit the fan in order to learn anything! Allow the lessons that you learn about yourself during your heyday♥ and the changes you make in your life during fun, fabulous, joyful moments build your character, help you figure out exactly what you want in life, and give you the confidence to get it.

The first step, as always, is to figure out precisely what you want. What kind of woman do you want to be—what sort of mark do you want to leave on this world? If you've never spent time thinking about this and have instead been making decisions blindly or out of routine, it's time to change that. You have the power to transform your life into the one you want. All you have to do is bust out any writing implement of your choice and create a Magical♥ Master Plan (MMP) for yourself, your heyday♥, and your entire life. Go somewhere quiet, take your time, dig deep, and don't be scared to write down your heart's deepest secrets and your mind's wildest dreams. Use this tool to put your heyday♥ to work for you and see how far you can go!

### *What Parts of My Life Do I Love?*
Take a moment to acknowledge all of the things in your life that are already working to make you happy. This can be your friends, your boyfriend, your job, or little things like drinking coffee in the morning while you watch the sun rise. Before you make any changes, it's important to honor the things that are already perfect and appreciate everything you have, so take this opportunity to do that right here.

_____

_____

_____

_____

_____

_____

_____

_____

### What Parts of My Life Do I Want to Change?

Okay, now it's time to address the things in your life that you *don't* love. Do you hate your leaking, moldy apartment or need more positive people in your life? Are you sick and tired of your dead-end job, or do you wish that you had a better relationship with your mother-in-law? Before you take action, write down exactly what you want to change and it will help you make it happen.

_____

_____

_____

_____

_____

_____

_____

_____

_____

_____

_____

### What Is Most Important to Me in Life?

Is it family, friends, living somewhere exotic, changing the world, or money? (Be honest.) What are your priorities? Is it more important to you to have easy hours and tons of vacation time or a high salary and work that you care about? Would you trade everything to live by the ocean or sacrifice financial security in order to pursue your greatest passion? Write down what is most important to you and we promise that your destiny will become much clearer.

_____

_____

_____

_____

_____

_____

_____

_____

_____

_____

_____

### *Who Do I Want to Be?*

This is major: how do you want to be remembered and thought of when you're not around? Do you want to be a kind, nurturing mother and friend, or a revolutionary who changed the world? Do you want to be a tough, savvy businesswoman, or a carefree, open-hearted artist? Do you want to be the shoulder your friends always cry on, someone who is open with her feelings and emotions, or self-sufficient and detached? You can be whoever it is you want to be, so think for a moment and write down exactly who that is.

_____

_____

_____

_____

_____

_____

_____

_____

_____

_____

### *How Can I Use My Heyday♥ to Create My Dream Life?*

It helps, but it's not enough to just write down what you want; you need a plan to go out and get it! How are you going to use this wonderful heyday♥ of yours to make all these changes? Are you going to apply for new jobs on your lunch break, network your ass off at parties, or finally start online dating so that you can find the love you deserve? Come up with a few ways that you are going to actively make your life better and write them down so that you don't forget!

_____

_____

_____

_____

_____

_____

_____

_____

_____

_____

### What Does My Dream Life Look Like?

Instead of writing for this part, we want you to tap into your inner Martha Stewart (minus the ice queen thing, please) and get all crafty with it. Just like how women in the '80s taped pictures of Jane Fonda to their fridges to help them lose weight and books like *The Secret* say to create a Vision Board to make your dreams come true, we want you to use your MMP to visualize your dream life. Pick a space anywhere you like (in a notebook, on your fridge, on a bulletin board over your desk, or whatever works for you) and cover it with pictures and words that represent the life you just described for yourself above.

Find pictures of the things you just told the universe♥ that you already love in your life (a photo of you and your best friend or your company's logo), add images that symbolize your new priorities (a dollar bill or a picture of your family), include something that embodies the woman you want to be (maybe it's our definition of a Hot Chick or the picture of the girl on the cover of this book), and finally add pictures of the things you are going to do during your heyday♥ to make this all come true (your online dating profile, a picture of a martini glass, or anything else that speaks to you). The only part of the MMP that you need to leave out is the stuff you said you want to change about your life; this is about putting your deepest dreams and truest desires in pictures where you can see them every day until they're a part of your life, and until eventually they *are* your life. Facing your dreams like this will serve as a constant reminder to focus on your goals and will magically♥ force the universe♥ to deliver them to you all tied up in a giant, shiny bow.

# Life's Little Surprises

Once you're done with the MMP, all you have to do is put it in a safe place and keep it in the back of your mind so that you can refer to it if you're ever feeling uninspired or LSE♥. Never forget that you deserve everything you just told the universe♥ that you wanted (unless you asked for magical powers or something). Not believing that you deserve something is often what prevents you from getting it, so listen to the good people at L'Oréal and remember that "you're worth it." Now that you've been clear with the universe♥ about all this, it knows what to give you, so just stay positive and keep on living like the Hot Chick that you are by enjoying every moment of your heyday♥. It will be so much fun to look back on your MMP in a year or three and see how much positive change you've accomplished.

Keep in mind that your life may not look exactly like the one you asked for, but that doesn't mean it isn't for the best. Just as rules are meant to be broken, plans are meant to be deviated from sometimes, so don't take this whole thing too literally. It is simply a blueprint that can evolve and change—often for the better. We hated that movie *The International*, but it did have one great quote: "Sometimes you find your destiny on the path you took trying to avoid it." We want you to remember that quote when you think about your goals in life. It's important to have dreams and a plan for reaching them, but it's equally essential to know that it's okay if things don't turn out the way you expected.

You may intentionally change your path one day and then end up right back where you started. You might follow your MMP to the letter and it might take you somewhere you never would have imagined in your wildest dreams. You just need to embrace the concept of the unknown as a beautiful thing, and while you're making the most of your heyday♥, keep yourself open to the exciting curveballs that life might throw at you. You may think you want to be married for three years before you start a family, but you may get knocked up tomorrow. You may have asked for a gym membership that you can't afford yet and start hiking instead, and end up crossing paths (literally) with your new best friend. Or you might want a new job and decide to focus on your career instead of relationships for the next year—and end up meeting your soul mate during an interview.

You can find your true destiny in unexpected ways by following your MMP but allowing for some flexibility along the way. When we completed our own MMPs, we never thought to write down that we wanted to help women feel like the Hot Chicks that they are, but we took a diversion to find out that this was our destiny—and we're so grateful that we did.

# Chapter 10

## Celebrate Your Life

WHEN WE'RE BUSY WITH WORK AND FAMILY OBLIGA-
TIONS, SPECIAL OCCASIONS CAN IRONICALLY CREATE
MORE ANXIETY AND OWL♥ THAN EXCITEMENT AND
ANTICIPATION. Many of us even become tempted to skip celebrations because it's easier to stay home; while it's certainly ac-
ceptable to turn down invitations when you need a break, in order
to truly enjoy and make the most of your life, you need to embrace
it and celebrate it every chance you get.

We know how stressful celebrations can be. They use up two
of our most precious commodities—time and money—but the
truth is that they are worth it. Weddings, baby showers, birthday
parties, vacations, and holidays all take planning, money, and energy away from the rest of our lives, but they also supply us with
laughter, inspiration, and fun memories that help keep us going. If
you shit all over celebrations by making them stressful, you need
to know that the rest of your life will suffer, too. Your foonge face♥

will eventually lead to depression, a lack of invitations, and deep-set frown wrinkles—so you need to turn your frown and your attitude around.

If we didn't have special occasions to look forward to, what would be the point of working so hard? Wouldn't life feel far less meaningful without family gatherings and beach vacations? You only get *one* life, and we want you to live it basking in celebratory moments instead of avoiding them so that you don't smack yourself on the forehead on your deathbed and realize that you missed out on life. Get ready to celebrate your life in a way that will change your entire life—for the better.

# The Importance of Parties

Parties have been medically proven to be as essential for your health as going to the dentist every six months and getting your annual pap smear and mammograms *combined.* If you don't stimulate the part of your brain that lights up during joyful moments, you will need to find comfort in things that are destructive like crappy food, drugs, alcohol, or relationships with bad boys with BMS♥, so it's essential to your health that you nurture that part of your brain that needs to let loose and party!

Of course, going to a party isn't going to cure all of your ills, solve all your problems, or magically turn you into a joyous person, but filling your life with celebrations will give you something to look forward to, an excuse to socialize with other Hot Chicks, an opportunity to meet new people, and a reminder that life really can be fun. We're not talking about throwing your giant stack of bills out the window and partying every night—and if you're in college you probably don't exactly need a reminder to party—but if you've been working too hard and missing your heyday♥, you need to ignore the piles of laundry and soap scum in the bath tub for a minute and find an incentive to have fun. If you're lacking creativity, we'll make it easy on you with these ten reasons to throw a party right this very moment!

## 1—Look for Love
You're not going to meet the love of your life sitting alone, eating pizza on your couch (unless he's the delivery boy, but that sounds too much like the plotline of a porno). Anyway, your dream date, true love, hookup, or kissing buddy might just show up at the next

party you throw or attend, so stop waiting for someone else to do the work for you and throw one tonight!

## 2—Widen Your Network Net

If you're out of work or looking for a new job, there is no better reason to throw a party. You might meet your future boss or business partner over martinis and artichoke dip. Good things tend to bloom out of carefree, joyful moments, so turn sharing a glass of champagne and a chocolate-covered strawberry with someone into savvy business practice.

## 3—Multiply Your Invites

If your social calendar is looking a little . . . blank, the best way to fill it up is to throw a party. Everyone you invite will make sure to include you the next time *they* throw a party, you'll meet new people at their parties who will all invite you to *their* next parties, and on and on until you can't possibly party any more.

## 4—Let Yourself Eat Cake

You will always have our permission to eat cake, but there is no better reason than throwing a party. If you're one of those Hot Chicks who claims to hate cake, we don't totally believe you, but we'll allow you to substitute with any other food that makes your eyes light up, like guacamole, cheesy dip, or brownies.

## 5—Play Dress Up

Most of us have loved playing dress up since we were wee little chicks and our favorite thing to do was put on our mothers' lipstick and high heels. Well, throwing a party is the best excuse on the planet to tap into your inner beauty queen and buy a new dress or wear something that you've been dying to wear but is completely inappropriate for any other occasion than a party in your very own home.

### 6—Keep It Clean

Sometimes the only thing that motivates us to clean up is the fear of someone else seeing how we actually live, and the best way to keep our home neat and tidy is to have people over and force ourselves to keep it together. By deciding to have a party, you're basically deciding to scrub your place, which is a good thing; a clutter-free life means a clutter-free brain. Just remember that after the party you'll probably have to clean again—at least if it's a good one.

### 7—Keep Friends Close

The more full our lives become, the harder it is to find time for our friends. Gone are the days when we spent all afternoon hanging out and eating frozen yogurt, and we miss the bonding, fun, and laughter that came along with that. We've discovered that the best way to see our friends on a regular basis is to continuously throw and attend planned parties that we can all mark down on our calendars. If your friends are drifting apart, plan a party that will keep them close to your heart.

### 8—Make Others Happy

Throwing a party not only brightens your own life, but brings joy to everyone you invite, too! Your party will subconsciously encourage them to celebrate their own lives and inspire them to throw parties of their own. The more of us we have in celebratory mode, the happier and hotter everyone will be.

**9—Stay Indoors**

There is nothing better than being able to see friends and socialize on a snowy, cold, or rainy day without having to step foot outdoors. If you hate trekking out in winter, throw a holiday party and make all of your friends come to you! Not only will you stay warm and toasty, but you can wear skimpy clothes, heels that you can't walk three feet in, and an outrageous hairstyle that would be ruined by a winter hat. Genius!

**10—You Don't Need a Reason**

You may have noticed that we skipped all of the obvious things, and that's because you don't really need a reason to throw a party. Sure, you can celebrate a birthday, your promotion, a house warming, or the beginning of summer, but at the end of the day, life itself is enough of a reason to celebrate. Go ahead and throw a party to celebrate not having a reason at all!

# How to Throw a Party Like a Hot Chick

Now that you have your reason (or none at all), it's time for party planning! With our simple techniques and brainstorms for fun and easy food, drinks, decorations, and wardrobe for every type of party on the planet, you'll be able to throw any of them flawlessly. Don't stress about being a perfect hostess; just settle down and let our party-throwing tips inspire you to create a party of your own.

## Holiday Hooplas

It's a great idea to pick one (or two!) of your favorite holidays of the year and throw an annual party on that day. That way, all of your friends will plan on attending and you'll avoid throwing conflicting, cock-blocking parties with each other or anything messy like that. For example, we throw an annual St. Paddy's Day party (and we're not even the slightest bit Irish). We serve Irish car bombs, green apple martinis, and green frosting-filled cupcakes, and the debauchery is a blast every year! Pick your own favorites and create a tradition that everyone you know will be able to look forward to.

*Food:* We think the cheesier the better, and we're not just talking about fondue. Bake football-shaped cookies for a Super Bowl party, a bunny cake for Easter, heart-shaped pizzas and red velvet cupcakes for Valentine's Day, spaghetti "intestines" and ghost-shaped cookies for Halloween, and enchiladas and guacamole for Cinco de Mayo. Get creative and have fun with it and your guests will, too! Plus, making food fun and celebratory brings everything together—your heyday ♥, your new celebratory outlook on life, and the end of your issues with food.

*Drinks:* Again, match your beverages to the holiday. Pink champagne is great for Valentine's Day, have spiked eggnog at a Christmas Party, make margaritas for Cinco de Mayo, and extra bloody Bloody Marys on Halloween.

*Decorations:* A few little touches will go a long way to make people feel cozy and ready to party. Buy cheap balloons in colors that match your holiday or in the colors of the two Super Bowl teams and tie them in bunches around your house, carve jack-o'-lanterns and fill them with candles to create a spooky Halloween theme, or fill bowls with pastel-colored candies on Easter and blue and white M & Ms for Chanukah.

*Wardrobe:* You are the Hot Chick hostess, and you should go all out for your role. Don't be afraid to wear a Santa hat, bunny ears, a clown costume, or a silver sequined gown.

## Barbeque Blowouts

Barbecues are great because it's hard to be mad or stressed out when you're biting into a juicy cheeseburger and drinking a cold beer while surrounded by cool people and bathed in sunshine. Remember, you don't need to have a giant backyard with an infinity pool in order to have a great BBQ. It can be just as cool to grill out on the fire escape of your apartment or grab a picnic table and grill at the park!

*Food:* If you're on a budget, it's fine to stick with hamburgers and hot dogs, but chicken and fish are great on the grill, too. Either way, don't forget your veggies! We like to grill skewers of red onion, zucchini, mushrooms, and colorful peppers, and of course some corn on the cob. (Keep floss handy.) For the vegetarians, please skip those hockey-puck-style frozen veggie burgers and grill up some juicy Portobello or eggplant slices (or make your own veggie burgers if you feel like channeling your inner Top Chef). Skip the mayo-laden potato and pasta salads that nobody really likes and make a giant spinach salad and chocolate chip cookies, instead.

*Drinks:* Save money by using cheap wine to make sangria! Pour the wine in a jug, chill it, and let it sit for several hours with slices of lemons, oranges, and maybe even some pineapple. Also, Benjamin Franklin said, "Beer is proof that G*d loves us and wants us to be happy," and we couldn't agree more, so always have some beer chilling in the cooler. Finally, pick one type of hard liquor and the corresponding ingredients to mix it with: tequila and limes for margaritas, rum and mint for mojitos, or gin and tonic for . . . gin and tonics! (Oh, and it's always a good idea to have some plain iced tea and lemonade on hand for people who may be secretly pregnant, in AA, super religious, or choosing not to imbibe for some other reason.)

*Decorations:* You don't need shit! How sweet is that?

*Wardrobe:* It's your party, so you can wear whatever you want, but we love the fact that a barbecue means that you can get away with anything from ripped jeans and flip-flops to a fun, sexy sundress. Remember that you set the tone for your own party, so wear whatever will put you and your guests in the mood to celebrate!

## Birthday Bashes

We are giving you permission right here and right now to throw your own birthday party. This is your heyday♥, and no matter how old you are turning, you should always celebrate the day that you were born into this awesome universe♥! Also, remember that it's better to give than to receive; if you have the time and money, why not throw a birthday party for your man, one of your friends, a family member, or a coworker you genuinely like? If you do it right, it's actually *fun* to throw someone else a party, especially if you choose to throw a surprise party and shock the shit out of someone you love.

*Food:* You must have a birthday cake with candles or it's not a birthday party, so don't even think about skimping on that. If you want to have birthday brownies or a birthday pie or some shit, we will allow that, but only if there are candles and you actually sing the song, otherwise it doesn't count. If it's your party, you get to have whatever food your pretty heart desires. Make some fun appetizers like cheesy spinach and artichoke dip, spicy walnuts, and tons of cheese and crackers—if you don't feel like cooking, just buy one of those surprisingly good sheet cakes from Costco and call it a day. If you're throwing a party for someone else, make sure you have their favorite foods. That means don't serve chicken wings and mini-meatballs at your sister's party if she's a vegetarian, and if you're surprising your man with a birthday celebration, make sure you have plenty of sausages, Doritos, and ice cream sandwiches (or whatever it is he loves).

*Drinks:* Make a giant bowlful of punch beforehand, whether it's a fun, fruity punch or a fancy champagne punch. This is an easy way to give your guests something to drink without making them work for it. Make sure that the guest of honor (whether it's you or someone else) is toasting with their favorite beverage, be it mudslides, beer, wine, or screwdrivers. Since you're partying at home, you can get as hammered as you want; just be safe and make sure not to get into a car, a catfight, or the boxers of some random guy.

*Decorations:* You can get paper streamers at the ninety-nine-cent store, so go crazy and decorate your whole house for five dollars. Balloons are always good, flowers are especially nice, and in case you were curious, you're never too old for a party hat or a tiara!

*Wardrobe:* If you're throwing yourself a birthday party, you have our permission to go out and buy a new party dress. Set a budget ahead of time and obviously don't splurge if you really can't afford it, but this is a great birthday present for yourself that will make you feel like a Hot Chick at your own party—as you should.

## Girly Gatherings

These include bridal showers, baby showers, slumber parties, bachelorette parties, clothing swap parties, sex toy parties, and any other party you can think of that gets you and your Hot Chicks friends together for a celebration. As much as we love men, they can be smelly and annoying, and sometimes it's nice to get away and party with just the gals. It will make you feel grateful for all of the awesome ladies you have in your life and inspire you to keep on living like a Hot Chick.

*Food:* It's so great to not have to cater to the guys so that you can have only the stuff that girls love, like cheese and chocolate. You can actually have only cheese and chocolate and most girls would be happy, but make sure to stick with the theme of your party at least a little bit. If you're throwing bridal shower, get cupcakes or M&Ms in the bride's wedding colors, and if it's a bachelorette party, please don't shy away from a giant penis-shaped cake!

*Drinks:* If your friend is having twins, throw her a baby shower with both sparking blueberry juice and sparkling pink lemonade. Make cosmos or Bellinis for the sex toy party (everyone will need to loosen up), and always count on penis-shaped Jell-O shots for the bachelorette.

*Decorations:* You really have to go all out here; just remember how much fun these photos will be years from now. Search online for tons of cheap "Bride-to-be" stuff for bridal showers or decorate with the wedding colors. Blue and pink are always good for baby showers (or yellow if they're keeping the gender a surprise). We know it's overkill with the penises, but they make penis everything nowadays (straws, plates, chip and dip dishes, macaroni, etc.), and you'll never have another excuse to buy this stuff, so just stop fighting it and do it. Don't forget about party favors when buying your decorations. Pick up some cheap candy necklaces, panties, and lip glosses, and make adorable little girly gift bags for all of your Hot Chick friends.

*Wardrobe:* Sundresses are ideal for bridal or baby showers, but for the sexier soirées, it can be really fun to get all dolled up for just the girls. Put on your most risqué, sexy outfits and see how much fun it is to dress this way and not have to worry about getting weird attention from skeezy guys!

# Vacations Are Vital

Celebrating life is not just about throwing parties, drinking martinis, and eating cake! Getting away from it all to take a simple vacation (or to travel extensively) is an essential way to celebrate your life. Vacations truly are vital to living, feeling, and playing like a Hot Chick, and it's important to get away from your physical space as often as you can. Whether it means travelling to another city, state, country, or continent, you need to break out of the monotony and learn about how the rest of the world lives. Travelling will force you to learn new things about yourself while teaching you new and exciting things like languages, customs, and the differences between champagne, cava, and sparkling California wines.

Plus, as great as it is to get away from your stacks of bills and piles of laundry, traveling truly does help you appreciate your home sweet home. Taking a vacation, no matter how big or small, is a way to recharge your mind, body, and sprit. You'll return to real life revitalized and inspired to live to the fullest. However, you have to plan it right because if done improperly, travel can totally backfire. We don't want you to end up sleeping in a roach-infested hostel or eating KFC in Paris, so follow our trusty travel trips to save yourself from disappointments, stress, and quite a few intestinal difficulties.

**Trusty Travel Tips**

**1—Pack Smart**

Don't bring everything in your closet with you on vacation including the stuff you don't like. The point is to get away from it all, not to take it all with you. Plus, now that the greedy airlines are charging for checked bags, there is a financial benefit to packing smart. Think about where you're going and plan it out; if you're going somewhere warm, bring casual shorts, tanks, and T-shirts for each day plus a fun going out outfit for each night, but be smart and pack things that you can wear over and over again like your magic♥ jeans, black pants, and neutral tops that go with everything. And we are hereby limiting you to four pairs of shoes—that includes flip-flops. There is no need to schlep a pair of bright pink heels that only go with one outfit or plastic thigh-high f-me boots, so stick with basics like black or silver heels, one comfy pair of sneaks, and shoes for the beach. Whoever's carrying your luggage will thank you later, *especially* if that's you. Spice things up with fun accessories that don't take up space like hats, scarves, and earrings, and never forget the lingerie (which is better the less space it takes up)!

### 2—Turn off the BlackBerry

Okay, we know that sometimes you need to check in with work, but if we find out that you're sending tons of emails from your BlackBerry on the beach or running back to the room every ten minutes to check your Facebook page, we are going to find you and kick your pretty little butt! You are not giving your brain the recharge that it needs if it's constantly connected to cyber space. We will allow you to check your email exactly once a day and use the Internet for vacation-related activities only, like looking up restaurants on Trip Advisor or making museum reservations. Trust us, you'll have plenty of time for the Web when you get back home, so take a break while you can!

### 3—Tell Someone Where You Are

Before you leave, give your parents, your best friend, and maybe even someone at work your flight and hotel information so that they can find you if they need to. This will help you relax on vacation and assuage the need to constantly check in to see if everything's okay at home—if something goes wrong, you'll hear about it, so you can relax! Plus, you need to be safe, especially if you're travelling alone (which we highly recommend). The world is a wonderful place to explore, but there are a ton of crazies out there filling it up. Put your mind (and your mom's) at rest by making your whereabouts known.

### 4—Avoid Chains at All Costs

It may seem like a safe, money-saving move to stay at a Hilton, Marriot, or Best Western wherever you go, but there are so many unique, more interesting accommodations out there that are actually way cheaper. Look into bed and breakfasts, boutique hotels that are willing to negotiate, and even apartment rentals! Call the establishment and ask them to match the Hampton Inn's rate and we bet they will. This will give you a much more uncommon experience than staying somewhere that will only add more money to Paris Hilton's trust fund.

### 5—Keep a Journal

Document your trip with as many photos as humanly possible, but also keep a journal of your innermost thoughts about your travels. When you're back at home in the midst of your regular life, it will be so much fun to look back on how much liberating fun you were having on vacation. Reading your account of the cute waiter, the peaceful feeling of the ocean's waves, or how the maid walked in on you and your boyfriend in a very precarious position will make you smile and giggle way more than any tacky souvenir.

### 6—Prepare Yourself

The more time you spend doing research before your trip, the more fun you will have on it, plain and simple! We know some of you are super spontaneous (and we totally support that), but if you take off to Mexico with nothing more than a jean skirt and tiny pink tank top with seventy-two dollars in your bra, you're totally being a dingbat. You need to plan out your trip for your safety and your sanity. Spend some time researching hotels, making dinner reservations, and making sure that you understand the transportation system and laws of the land so you don't end up on *Locked Up Abroad!* (P.S. If you are even *considering* strapping cocaine to your thighs, you kind of deserve a lifetime locked up in a feces-smeared cell. Don't be stupid, Hot Chicks!)

### 7—Eat Local Food

If we find out that you are dining at Chili's and Subway on your vacation, we will not be your friends anymore. Your vacation is an opportunity to explore and learn about the world, and hard as you try, you really can't do that at the Taco Bell drive-through. Eat exclusively at local, non-chain restaurants, and make it a rule that you will try one new food every single day of your trip, even if it's something that scares the crap out of you like fried sand eels. Your palette, your journal, and your future memories will all be grateful.

### 8—Stick to a Budget

So many people lose all self-control when they're on vacation and start doing crazy shit like eating out the entire mini-bar every night, ordering Oysters Rockefeller at each meal, and buying overpriced souvenirs that are doomed to become clutter. We want you to have a good time and we know that will cost money, but you need to keep it together. The best way to do that is to set a budget beforehand. Decide how much you can spend on your trip, whether it's five thousand dollars on your honeymoon or forty dollars a day like poor Rachael Ray did on that Food Network show before she was super famous, and stick to that number!

Decide what is most important to you and spend money on that, whether it's nice meals out, room service, or tons of new Italian leather. Just don't go overboard, or this might be the last vacation you ever take.

### 9—Try out the Language

Okay, ignore this one if you're staying stateside, but if you're going anywhere from Quebec to Uganda, you should really try to muster up a few basic words like "hello," "please," and "thank you" in the native tongue. It will broaden your mind, endear you to the locals, and do worlds of good for the crappy reputation of Americans around the globe!

### 10—Go with Your Gut

The most important thing you can do on your trip is to get home safe! We don't care if Frommer's says that the best restaurant in town is down that dark, desolate alley; if it looks sketchy, don't go there! The same thing goes for interacting with the locals. We are all for you flirting it up with cute local boys, but don't turn a fun heyday♥ experience into a true tragedy by going home with a stranger or trusting anyone you don't know. You are in charge of your mind, heart, and body, and you need to be alert when you're somewhere unfamiliar. Always put safety first—even when you're getting a piece—so that you can get home in one piece!

# Money-Saving Moves

The number one thing that keeps us from taking those vital vacations is often money, or the lack thereof, but vacations don't have to always be expensive. We've found a few foolproof ways to save thousands on a trip, so start looking into these or let them inspire you to find your own way to get away without breaking the bank.

### 1—Friends with Benefits

Use your friends to share costs on a vacation that you otherwise wouldn't have been able to afford. Rent a condo on the beach, carpool there, and cook dinner each night, and it will add up to so much less than the cost of getting a hotel room and eating out every night. Alternatively, if you have a friend who lives in another city, use your vacation time to visit her! Flying to Rome and crashing on your friend's couch might actually be cheaper than driving to the shore and staying at a hotel, and will probably end up being even more fun.

*Note: If you're splitting the condo, remember that cooking for all those people requires a ton of prep work and dishwashing time, so make sure your brain is wired to do a little housework on vacation and always do your part. And if you're staying with a friend, make sure to bring her a gift or take her out to dinner as an act of gratitude for putting you up, and you'll be much more likely to be invited back!*

### 2—All About All-Inclusive

It is an incredible feeling to pay one fee for your flight, hotel, food, drinks, and all sorts of extra goodies, and then pay absolutely nothing once you start your vacation. It's so liberating to sit down to dinner and order whatever you want without thinking about cost, or to be able to go jet skiing without handing over your Visa. Some of these places will restock your mini-bar every morning for free or even include free massages. Doesn't that sound like heaven? Some of these packages are expensive, but many aren't when you add up what you would end up paying for everything separately, so quit ignoring those cheesy ads for Sandals, do some research, and think about going all-inclusive on your next trip!

*Note: Sometimes the food at all-inclusive resorts isn't as yummy as it looks, so get creative to give yourself more variety. Skip the cold, oily scrambled eggs at the breakfast buffet and order a mango margarita and a cheeseburger by the pool. It will be calories, stomach space, and free meals better spent.*

### 3—Bid, Gamble, and Save

We once went to Priceline.com, bid on a random hotel, and surprised ourselves by getting a room at a five-star hotel for the cost of a Super 8! Check out these chances to bid on vacations and don't be afraid to be bold. You might end up on a seven-day cruise for fifty bucks just because nobody else bid on it. Of course, be smart and do your research beforehand, or you might end up paying way too much to stay somewhere really shady—but if you do it right, this can be a great way to get away while simultaneously getting an adrenaline high from scoring a major deal.

*Note: Please don't just start plugging your credit card number into every travel Web site you find. That's a recipe for disaster.*

### 4—Time-Share Technique

We think that sitting through a three-hour sales pitch for a time-share is totally worth a free vacation. Sure, it's a little naughty, but everyone else does it, so why shouldn't you? Plus, who's to say that you won't actually make a time-share purchase in a few years' time? (Wink, wink.) If you can handle intense mental pressure and intimidation techniques from salesmen who have an MBA in preying on your LSE♥, enjoy your free trip.

*Note: This will undoubtedly go down as heyday♥ experience.*

**5—Negotiate Your Power**
Sometimes in order to get what you want in life, all you have to do is ask. Don't settle for paying the sticker price on anything, even your vacations. Strap on your balls and call the airlines, hotels, and car rental places and tell them how much you want to spend. You'll be surprised by how many things in life are more negotiable than you thought! (Well, maybe not flights, but if they keep on losing money, we think that the airlines should learn to negotiate, too.)

*Note: As in any negotiation, you have to be willing to walk away, so always make sure that you have a backup plan just in case. You don't want to book a hotel in some random city and then start negotiating for the only flight there that day or you won't have much "walk away power" to negotiate with!*

# Celebrate Downtime

In order to truly play like a Hot Chick and find the peace of mind to celebrate your life, you need to schedule some downtime for yourself. Quiet time is essential so that you can reflect on your life, make plans, set goals, and relive every juicy moment that you've had so far. So many of us move full steam through our lives, multitasking every moment away without a quiet moment away from it all, and many of us even feel guilty and spoiled for craving downtime. Well, that is no way to live, and over time it will only end up intensifying the wrinkles on your permanent foonge♥ face. We know how hard it is to find free time, but we promise that if you make it a priority and schedule it in, you'll be a hotter Hot Chick for it. Check out our L-E-I-S-U-R-E list of seven tips that will help you balance your life, stay sane, and celebrate in a way that's more revitalizing than a triple oxygen peel followed by a triple-shot Americano.

## L—Learn to Say, "NO"

We know that we just spent the majority of this book encouraging you to always accept invitations and say yes to things the universe♥ offers you, but it is equally important to know when it's time to say no. The quickest way to get more downtime for yourself is to decline things that you know will drain you, whether that's an invitation to your nemesis's holiday party, an opportunity to run the school bake sale, or a plea by your ex to pick him up from the airport. This is *your* life, and it's okay to say no to other people sometimes to make room for you! Take control, start saying no, and see how liberated and relaxed you feel.

### E—Enjoy the Moment

When you go somewhere you like, do you find yourself thinking things like, *"I can't wait to come back here?"* It's great to make future plans, but in order to find peace of mind, you have to start living in the moment. That means thinking about nothing but where you are, the things around you, and every sensation in your body—from the way the wind hits your face to the taste of your wine and the smell of fresh air. This moment is all you really have, so enjoy it while it lasts, Hot Chicks!

### I—Idle Away Your Weekend

There is no law that says you have to have impressive plans on Friday and Saturday nights, so try to spend one weekend a month doing not much of anything. Sleep in, rent videos, organize your photos, cook three-course meals for yourself; do whatever sounds like fun in the moment. It's amazing how much you can learn about yourself by forcing yourself to fill up an empty weekend.

### S—Sleep In

Did you see that Oprah episode where she said that she always gets up early just because she "feels like she should"? Did you relate to this as much as we did? (We love you, Oprah!) Let yourself sleep as late as you can on one day over the weekend, and if you accidentally wake up early, just lie there and relax completely, enjoying the feeling of doing nothing at all. Don't feel guilty about sleeping late! How else are you going to recover from the fast pace you keep the rest of the time?

### U—Unplug

Leave your phone at home and go for a walk, turn your computer off for the entire weekend, or go without TV for a while. Most of us spend far too much time staring at glowing screens to possibly relax, so unwind by unplugging your devices and setting yourself free from the constant buzz of texts, emails, calls, and chats. Just try this and see how much more refreshed you feel when you boot back up on Monday.

## R—Read a Good Book

If you take the subway or bus to work or school, let someone else's story magically turn your annoying, sweaty, dirty, long commute into a leisure time that you will actually start looking forward to. Give your brain a break and read a few pages on your lunch break or unwind at night by reading just before falling asleep. Use books to transport yourself away from the stress of your life and into someone else's—your own struggles are sure to seem a lot more manageable.

## E—Eat Slowly

Stop eating dinner in front of the TV, eating lunch at your desk while checking emails at work, and eating breakfast by letting go of the steering wheel for a minute to reach into a cereal box on the passenger seat. Turn mealtime into leisure time by skipping the multitasking and doing nothing but eating. Savor your food and be in the moment. You'll not only enjoy it a whole lot more, but you'll fill up quicker and end up more satisfied when it's over. Your taste buds, stress level, and waist line will all be better for it.

# Chapter 11

## *Friends and Family*

NO MATTER HOW GOOD A JOB YOU DO OF BALANCING THE REST OF YOUR LIFE, THE PEOPLE YOU SURROUND YOURSELF WITH CAN MAKE OR BREAK THAT BALANCE. Your relationships with family members and friends help determine your general level of happiness and influence the way you actually live your life. If you spend all of your time with negative, depressed, pessimistic people, it is nearly impossible not to start to feel that way, too, but choosing carefully who you spend your precious time and energy on will help you feel inspired, energized, and positive about life. How you behave in these relationships is just as important. If you act LSE♥ around your best friend and bratty around your family, your bad energy will rub off on them, bounce back onto you, and destroy these relationships.

Have no fear—we are going to teach you how to pick your friends much more carefully than you pick your split ends and tell you how to nourish your relationships with the people you are stuck with (your family) so that time together doesn't feel quite so much like a jail sentence. If you are sidetracked by a friend whose risky behavior always gets you in trouble or losing beauty sleep over ugly arguments with your father, we can help you. Although parasitic people will always find a way into your life, we'll help you recognize the a-holes, b-words, and even c-words, and give you clever ways for cutting them off so that you are left with only people in your life who will help you shine.

# Family First

You are just one small but unique branch of a giant family tree that has thick roots around the world. There's nothing you can do to stop being a part of your family. You can divorce them, move to another continent, and cut off all communication, but you'll still have their hot blood running through your veins. (And if you were adopted, you have twice as many roots!) Although you can't choose your family, you can choose how you deal with them. Whether your family gets along great or trying to make peace with your family is like trying to reason with a great white shark (i.e., impossible), we can all use some extra tips on how to help these relationships thrive. That's because of a strange phenomenon common to many families when they all get together—everyone magically♥ turns into a bratty fifteen-year-old. You may have blacked it out, but we can vaguely remember being fifteen and trying to get along with other fifteen-year-olds, and it wasn't pretty. There are a lot of tantrums, eye rolling, foonge faces♥, and heart-wrenching blowouts involved, all of which end up making you feel like a giant piece of dog shit when it's over.

Family feuds may seem as harmless and normal as high school drama, but they can be more damaging than you realize. Letting yourself spiral out of control around your family will only make you feel misunderstood and alone when you're with the very people who are supposed to know you best in the world. This in and of itself is frustrating, exhausting, and depressing, and so you have to prevent the people you love from bringing out the worst in you. We know that there are some really screwed up families out there, and if your dad was Charles Manson or your mom is Candy Spelling, it might just be better for you to cut them off completely—but all of our families are fucked up♥ and crazy in their own, unique ways. They are all human with their own flaws and self-doubts, and as we get older it's easier to see that the fights we've had with our parents may have stemmed from their own LSE♥, OWL♥, or regrets.

It will help you get along with your family to realize that they are people, too, with their own hearts, minds, desires, wishes, and disappointments. They love you unconditionally, but they had lives before you came along, and those lives made them who they are. They may not act exactly the way you'd like them to, but it's not always about you, Hot Chicks! Why don't you try showering them with love instead of trying to turn them into different people, and healing their LSE♥ with kind words instead of saying hurtful things that will only make it worse? You must do everything in your power to get along with your family, because at the end of the day, they're all you have. You can find another group of friends, but you can't go out and get another family. If you don't genuinely try to make your relationship with this one work, you will regret it, and regret is something we wouldn't wish on our worst enemy (not even those Skinny Bitches). If you don't know where to start, we're going to give you a few examples of how to love your family even when you feel like you hate them.

# Ten Sticky Family Situations (and How to Deal with Them)

**Family Feud #1**—Your mom makes you feel like shit for being single.

*Family Fix*—There is nothing worse than finally enjoying your heyday♥ just to have your mom make cutting remarks over the Thanksgiving turkey about wanting to have grandchildren before she dies. The thing to remember here is that, although she is communicating it terribly, she really does want what's best for you. She wants you to be happy, and (unfortunately for her) her only association with "happy" is married. Let it go, but also let her know that you don't appreciate these comments in a kind and loving way. Try saying, "Mom, I am looking forward to meeting the perfect person when the time is right, but right now I am happy being single. Please don't try to make me feel bad, because I really am happy." Chances are that just hearing that you're happy will be enough to shut her up—at least for now.

**Family Feud #2**—Your grandma tells you that you are fat.

*Family Fix*—Any hint about weight from a family member can drive us to pour a boatload of gravy down our throats just to show them or go on a hunger strike all through the holidays. Again, remember that she really just wants the best for you, and it's not her fault that she has no bloody clue what the best for you actually is! Try saying something like, "Grandma, did you know that nowadays weight and body image issues are a problem for most women? Calling attention to my weight will only make me feel more insecure. Please just know that I am healthy and I am taking care of myself." She is from another generation, and once she knows this is a sensitive issue for today's Hot Chicks, she will (hopefully) stop.

**Family Feud #3**—Your dad still treats you like you're five years old.

    *Family Fix*—Although he managed to bag your mom, your dad might have no clue how to deal with women, and now that his baby girl has grown into a Hot Chick, he might be totally LSE♥ and confused about how to interact with you. Maybe he's just as tongue-tied around you as he is around all beautiful women. You need to help him out by talking to him like a normal person and showing him by example what kind of relationship you want to have. Call him up and ask about his day and tell him about yours. Open up about what's going on in your life and let him get to know the woman that you are. We're pretty sure that he'll be grateful to you for teaching him how to be a good dad, and that will bring you even closer.

**Family Feud #4**—Your family never says, "I love you."

    *Family Fix*—No matter how loving your family acts, it is amazing how not hearing these words can make you feel unloved. Remember that it doesn't mean they don't love you—they probably never learned how to show it from their own families and are unfortunately continuing this bad tradition. We think you should lead by example and just say it. Don't be LSE♥ or think it's a big deal. Say, "I love you" to your brother before hanging up the phone, write, "I love you" at the end of emails to your mom and letters to your grandma, and every time you see a family member, give them a big hug and say, "I love you." The best part is that it's not like saying it to a boyfriend where you don't have to worry about whether or not he'll say it back! Just speak your loving thoughts and stop letting LSE♥ stop you from being the most loving sister, daughter, niece, and cousin you can be.

**Family Feud #5**—Your cousin wears a white dress to your wedding.

    *Family Fix*—Just walk up to her with a glass of red wine and "accidentally" pour it all over her. No, just kidding; don't do that. You know what? She's obviously completely jealous of you and starved for attention. Don't waste one second or one iota of energy worrying about her on your special day. Trust us when we tell you that nobody is even giving her a second glance because they cannot peel their eyes away from you, you beautiful Hot Chick bride, you! Spend all of your time and energy enjoying every moment of your day, look back on it and laugh, and then mail your cousin a copy of this book!

**Family Feud #6**—Your favorite aunt voices disapproval of your sexual orientation, your new tattoo, or your nose ring.

    *Family Fix*—You can't please all the people all of the time, or even most of the people some of the time, and there is really no need to. As long as your behavior isn't hurting anyone, it's none of her damn business—but we know that doesn't make it any easier when someone you love makes nasty comments when all you want is her support. Try to get your aunt back on your side by saying something like, "I know this wouldn't be your choice, Aunt Lucy, and even though I made this choice, I am still the same person underneath. Having your love and support would mean the world to me." It may take a while for her to come around, but once she sees that you are the same loving niece as always, we're pretty sure she'll still want you in her life and stop acting like an idiot.

**Family Feud #7**—Your entire family hates your boyfriend.

*Family Fix*—This can be so hard, and if it happens to you, we are really sorry. There are few things that are worse than feeling torn between people you love. First of all, we totally trust you, but we want to make sure that your family isn't right, and that this guy is good enough for you. You can skip ahead to the end of the chapter to make sure you're in a healthy relationship. (We'll wait.) Okay, now that you've checked, sit your family down and open up to them; explain how loving and kind he is and tell them why you love him. Don't shy away from bringing him to family gatherings and just refuse to choose between them. We really hope that once they've gotten to know him, they will open their minds and eventually approve.

**Family Feud #8**—Your grandpa says sexist things all the time.

*Family Fix*—Your grandfather loves you, but he is from another generation, a time when things were completely different. Do you realize how much has changed for women since your grandfather was your age? He might have even been born before women in this country had the right to vote! We're not letting him off the hook for saying dumb, misogynistic crap, but it's important to know that no matter how many feminist rants you go on, you probably won't be able to change him. You can calmly voice your opinions or invent an urgent phone call that you have to make when he starts up, but save the hardcore debates for someone closer to your age who you might actually have a chance of convincing.

*Family Feud #9*—Your mom isn't very motherly; in fact, she's kind of cold.

*Family Fix*—We know you might feel like you missed out on motherly nurturing and that it's not fair, but there is nothing you can do to change that. Focus on how lucky you are for the things you have, instead, and remember that no family is perfect. Instead of letting your pain make you miserable, learn from it and let it make you more loving. Decide that you are going to be extra nurturing and warm to her, whether she accepts it or not, and remember that she is only like this because someone (her mother?) wasn't nurturing and loving enough with her. Have sympathy, not resentment, because it will be even harder for your mom to love you if you're a hater.

*Family Feud #10*—Your sibling acts really distant and you want to be close.

*Family Fix*—It's so easy to let the other person dictate with her actions which way a relationship is going to go. If your sister never reaches out and barely talks to you on Christmas, it can be tempting to just say, "Screw it; I guess we'll never be close," but we think you'll regret that in the long run. You decide what kind of relationship you want to have and then do whatever it takes to make it happen. Call your brother just to chat, even if it's awkward at first, and ask your sister about her life. Who knows? They might have wanted to be closer the whole time and were just being painfully LSE♥ and waiting for a sign from you.

# Toxic Friends

We hope you know what it feels like to have a good friend. You can laugh and celebrate life with her, cry on her shoulder without fear of judgment, and tell her your deepest secrets without feeling ashamed. She is always available for a pep talk, a venting session, or to support your decision to buy six new dresses. A good friend can make you feel like a Hot Chick who can accomplish anything even when you are completely LSE♥ and afraid, never acts jealous or competes with you for anything (a guy, a job, a wedding dress, or even just to be the "hot one"), and never lets you feel alone.

Those of us who are lucky will have a handful of these friends in our lives, and the rest of our circles will be made of decent friends, acquaintances, and inevitably some girls who we think are our friends but are actually toxic, unhealthy people who bring more trouble than they're worth into our lives. You probably have one or two of these bloodsuckers leeching your energy right now and you may not even know it! Sometimes a girl can start off as your absolute bestie and change over time into someone who competes with you, doesn't support you, and generally brings you down. Other friends may just be drains from the start, but you can't see it because you have such high hopes. Well, we want you to recognize these toxic bitches when you see them, because there is no room in your Hot Chick life for a friend who is more like an enemy. Pay close attention to these seven deadly signs that your friendship is more toxic than rat poison.

**Toxic Tipoff #1—Bitchy Borrower**
She is constantly borrowing money for lunch, clothes, movies, and even rent. She promises to pay you back, but she never seems to

get around to it. She always seems to be out of cash and asks you to spot her, but she never remembers to get you back next time (as promised). Deep down you feel a bit taken advantage of, but you're a little bit guilty about that because she's your friend—right? And money shouldn't come between friends. But if she keeps this up, she may not be your friend for long. Remember that your job as her friend is to support her emotionally, not financially. You are not her ATM, parent, or enabler, nor should you be.

**Toxic Tipoff #2—Just Jealous**
It may be your job, boyfriend, haircut, apartment, or trust fund, but this friend is jealous and competitive when it comes to all of the great things in your life and is never truly happy for you when good things happen. Jealous friends are dangerous because they can make you start to play small♥ around them and make light of the goodness in your life because you're afraid of . . . making her jealous! Well, she's the one making her jealous, not you, and you deserve a friend who celebrates your achievements right alongside you and never makes you feel weird about being happy.

**Toxic Tipoff #3—Callous and Cruel**
She is mean, condescending, and passive-aggressive, and the nasty things she says hurt you and make you doubt yourself. A friend should never badmouth another friend, either behind her back or to her face, and a girl who does this is obviously jealous, insecure, LSE♥, and not living like a Hot Chick. She may think she's getting the upper hand by putting you down, but she has no idea that her cutting words are actually just showing you (and everyone else) what a toxic, lousy friend she is.

## Toxic Tipoff #4—Overly Obsessive

She is possessive and jealous of your other friendships, secretly borrows your clothes and then never gives them back, asks for a key to your apartment, shows up everywhere you go, and throws a tantrum if you do anything fun without her. You think this friendship should feel sisterly, but it's starting to feel more and more insane. Well, we hate to be the one to tell you this, but she may be a total psycho, and you need to drop her faster than the guy who offered to buy you new boobs for your birthday so that you don't wake up one morning either with her in bed next to you or standing over you with a razor blade.

## Toxic Tipoff #5—Deadly Dread

When the phone rings and you see her name on the screen, your muscles tense up, you start grinding your teeth, and you'd rather throw your phone into speeding traffic than answer or ever call her back. This is a pretty sure sign that this friendship is over. In fact, every bit of your subconscious is working overtime to tell you that it's over, but you're hanging on because of some sense of obligation or guilt. Remember that friendships should be full of fun, not fear, and if you'd rather hear an ear-splitting fire alarm than the sound of her voice, you really need to listen to your intuition.

## Toxic Tipoff #6—Horrible Habits

She does things that make you uncomfortable, bring you down, and possibly make you look bad, like working at the only totally nude strip club in the country that serves alcohol, doing lines of coke in the bathroom at your friend's wedding, cheating on her husband, or cheating with a mutual friend's man. Even if these bad behaviors don't directly affect you, remember that who you spend your time with does tell the universe♥ a lot about you. Your friends should have, roughly, the same morals and values as you, not be people with lifestyles that you would never stoop to.

### Toxic Tipoff #7—Faulty Flirt

She may outright flirt with your man or just try to get sexual attention from him by casually sitting on his lap or saying inappropriate things around him like, "I went nude sunbathing today and I just love having no tan lines. It makes me horny." Saying this means that she wants your man to picture her naked, sunkissed, heydayish♥ vagina! Go back and reread the definition of a Hot Chick—remember that Hot Chicks never compete with each other, which is what flirting with each other's men really is. And we hope you get this by now, but you should only be friends with women who live up to that definition!

# Friends Forever?

If you recognized any of your friends in the descriptions above, don't worry. It's very common for a toxic person to snake her way into the life of a Hot Chick like you because she needs something positive in her life. It's fine to be needed, but when that neediness becomes toxic and damaging, it's time to let that person go. Many of us think that we'll be friends with our friends forever, but that's not necessary true. You may be lucky enough to have one or two lifelong besties, but the majority of friends come and go in and out of our lives and that's how it's meant to be. They each serve a purpose, whether it's to teach us something or share a particular time in our lives with, and then, after the relationship has run its course, you can both move on.

If you and a friend don't grow in the same direction or toxicity starts to creep into the friendship, it's time to cut the cord. Don't be afraid to cut people out of your life! You are a Hot Chick and you need to have high standards for your friends, just like the guys that you date and the jobs you take. Kicking toxic friends to the curb can be painful but incredibly liberating, kind of like how food poisoning makes you sick as a dog, but then, once the poison is out of your system, you feel even better than you did before. Okay, if that one didn't do it for you, it's like how cleaning out your closet is an arduous, annoying process that stirs up old memories that are hard to let go of, but once you drop off that trash bag at Goodwill, you feel free and light and like you have room in your life for cute new things that will make good new memories.

Liberating yourself from the burden of toxic friendships will help make room in your life for friends who support, encourage, and inspire you to continue being the Hot Chick that you are.

Because we're such good, non-toxic girlfriends, here are some ways to do that (in order of scariness).

**1—Cut the Cord and then Avoid**
Okay, this is kind of the wimpy way out, but whatever—it works. Just try not answering her calls one day, and then the next day don't call back, and then when she calls again on the third day don't answer again, and then don't call her back. You get the idea. We really only recommend using this technique if your "friend" did something truly horrible to deserve this kind of treatment, but sometimes just walking away from a bad thing without looking back is the best way to move forward.

**2—Mediate Your Break**
Find someone objective (a mutual friend or a role model, like a sorority leader or even a counselor) to be present when you confront your friend and tell her why you need a break from the friendship. It can be helpful to have a third party present to prevent it from getting ugly and to help you communicate through overflowing emotions. Remember not to attack her during this session; just clearly state why you can't be friends right now. If she freaks out, calls you names, spreads rumors, and acts like a bitch, she is only validating your decision.

**3—Put It in Print**
Don't go sending any hate mail, but writing a long letter explaining why you are ending a friendship is a good way to express yourself without letting the heat of the moment get in the way. It also eliminates the chance of her attacking you with gardening shears, a letter opener, or any other sharp object nearby. Be kind and clear in your letter and end the friendship with closure and a clear conscience.

**4—Give Her a Chance**

Maybe there are several problems in your friendship but you still think it's worth saving. In this case, you should definitely give it a chance, but you must take action to correct the things in your relationship that are wrong. Either write down or tell her by phone how important your friendship is to you, but let her know that you aren't happy with the way she treats your boyfriend or the comments she makes about your job. Tell her that these things must change in order for the friendship to continue, and if she gets mad, cuts you off, or just doesn't listen, you know what to do next . . .

**5—Face-to-Face**

This is tough, but you can do it! Sit your friend down and tell her that it's over and why. She may argue with you, get nasty, or just try to not let you break up with her, but you have to be strong and finish what you started. Don't let her manipulate you into apologizing for trying to call it quits or make you feel so guilty that you agree to take her back and give her another chance. Explain that you've already given her plenty of chances and that it really is over. Then email us and let us know how it went!

# Are You a Hot Chick Friend?

Before we move on, we want to make sure that you're not just cutting out the toxic friends in your life, but that you're also acting like a Hot Chick friend yourself in all of your friendships. If you recognized yourself in any of those toxic tip-offs (even a little bit), you need to get that shit in check. Friendships are delicate. They can be inspiring and life-enhancing if you treat them with dignity and respect, but they can turn ugly faster than Tiger Woods's reputation if you let jealousy, cattiness, or negativity take over. If more than one friend has kicked you to the curb or a bunch of your friends have tried to have some sort of friendship intervention with you, take that as a giant sign that you (gasp!) are a toxic friend yourself. Get it together and act like the Hot Chick that you are, or you will totally miss out by being unworthy of a beautiful, healthy friendship.

# Chapter 12

## Love Your Love Life

HAVING A HEALTHY, HAPPY LOVE LIFE IS A KEY IN-
GREDIENT IN A BALANCED HOT CHICK LIFE. If you are
in a messy, turbulent relationship, there's no way for you to feel
your best, and a stale, passionless romance can be just as draining.
Finding balance in the romance department is so important that
(as you already know) we wrote a whole book on it, but it completely relates to this book, too. How the hell can you live your life
to the fullest and take on the world like the Hot Chick that you
are when your heart is full of loneliness, sorrow, or fear instead of
passionate love?

We're not saying that you have to be in a relationship in order to live like a Hot Chick—quite the opposite! We want you
to enjoy every minute of your single heyday♥, your dating life,
or your comfy relationship so that you can go out into the world
feeling satisfied, nurtured, and loved. If you've never been in love,
then you're in for a real treat one day, and if you have, then you

know how a harmonious love life can help the other pieces of your life magically♥ fall into place. This goes for you single ladies, too! When you're content in your singlehood and confident that you'll find the right person when the time is right, everything else in your life will begin to make sense. But if you're tormented by a tumultuous romance or desperate to fall in love, it becomes that much more difficult to enjoy any part of your life.

In this chapter, we're going to teach you how to give your relationship the right amount of energy and attention so that you're nurturing your love without obsessing and open to finding love without feeling frantic. No relationship is perfect, but once you learn how to deal with the bickering and blowouts like the Hot Chick that you are, you'll be able to find yourself in the sweet spot of love far more often than the depths of despair.

# Dos and Don'ts to Loving Like a Hot Chick

Before we move on to fixing your relationship (or finding out if it needs fixing), we want to make sure that you are acting like a Hot Chick in your relationship. Healthy relationships require honesty, trust, flawless communication, devotion, thoughtfulness, respect, and a million other things like caring enough to not leave dirty dishes in the sink or beer bottle caps on the counter if you know it drives your lover insane. We want to make sure that you are doing all of these things as well as everything else in your power to make your relationship work. There will always be fights and setbacks and relationship perfection is pretty much impossible, but we still have to strive for it (kind of like how we try to get to the gym every day and only end up there a few days a week).

We want you to find the love you deserve, and since we can't change your man or drop one off at your doorstep (as much as we'd like to), our goal is to make sure that you are doing everything you can to attract a healthy love into your life. Follow our dos and don'ts so that you can spend less time in turbulent tornados and more time on cloud nine.

**Do #1—Compliment**
Tell your lover that he is sexy, smart, funny, and awesome! Don't lie or blow smoke, but there better be plenty of things that you like about him, so tell him what they are! Make him feel appreciated, loved, and lusted after, and he'll be so much more likely to do the same for you.

*Love Note: You may not believe it, but men are often more LSE♥ than we are! Boost his self-esteem with kind words and it will boost the overall health of your relationship.*

## Do #2—Make Time

Don't neglect the rest of your life, but don't let work, family, or friends become a higher priority than your relationship, either. Like a little seedling or a newborn, your relationship needs constant love and attention in order to bloom. Once Cupid has done his job by shooting you with his arrow, it's up to you to keep your love going strong. Make time together away from everything else a priority and your relationship will flourish like a beautiful rose.

*Love Note: Be careful not to let the little (or big) stresses of life come between you and your man. When you're feeling totally OWL♥, take a break, take a breath, and make sure not to take it out on your man!*

## Do #3—Compromise

You are not a princess who gets to have everything she wants without having to give up a little. You know the saying, "Happy wife = a happy life"? Well, the reverse is true, too. Small compromises on things like what to eat for dinner or what movie to see as well as bigger ones like where to spend the holidays and how many kids to have will all add up to a happier partner and a happier, healthier relationship.

*Love Note: Sex takes compromise, too, so be open to meeting in the middle when it comes to time, place, frequency, and even your level of kinkiness.*

## Do #4—Think before You Speak

No matter how angry or PMS-ie you are, you have no excuse for saying cruel things that you know will hurt your lover. Strategic biting of your tongue can be the deciding factor between homicide and living happily ever after.

*Love Note: Whatever idiot came up with the saying, "Sticks and stones may break my bones, but words will never hurt me" is a dumb ass. Words hurt really badly, so shut it before you ruin a good thing.*

## Do #5—Be Honest

Tell your man what you need from him to make you happy, whether it's chipping in with the housework or surprising you with flowers every so often. Keep it within reason, please, but don't be afraid to be honest. Your man will probably even be grateful to you for making his job easier by telling him exactly what you want.

*Love Note: Encourage your man to do the same thing and tell you what you can do to make him happier. Remember, it is your job to make each other happy, and you should take this job as seriously as one that pays in money instead of love.*

## Don't #1—Be a Stalker

Please don't act like a crazy bitch and check his phone, email, bank statements, or credit card bills, and don't follow him or drive past his house late at night. Remember that *Sex and the City* episode where Carrie was feeling LSE♥ and went through that guy's stuff? Well, please do yourself a favor and learn from her mistakes!

*Love Note: However, if he's given you a reason not to trust him, either by lying about his whereabouts or actually cheating, you might need to rethink this relationship. If your man's actions are making you crazy, we're very sorry, but there's not much hope that your love will survive the insanity. You deserve better and it's out there.*

### Don't #2—Smother

You can smother each other with kisses, but that's it. Don't insist on spending 24/7/365 together or you will scare him away faster than if you start talking about your ovulation cycle. Make sure that you have other things going on in your life that excite you and encourage him to do the same thing. Depending on each other is fine, but smothering and becoming codependent will leave you as out of balance as Amy Winehouse.

*Love Note: It's true—absence makes the heart grow fonder. Doing things separately during the day will help you appreciate each other more when you reunite at night.*

### Don't #3—Cheat

Instead of poking around in another yard, you need to focus on what's going on at home so that you can fix it instead of acting like a lazy, deceptive, and unfaithful bitch by letting another man poke you.

*Love Note: However, if you are actually pretty damned sure that the other grass is in fact greener and the grass at home is looking increasingly dry and brittle, end your relationship before starting a new one. A dying relationship is still no excuse to cheat!*

### Don't #4—Use Sex as a Weapon (or a Present)

The last time we checked, women enjoyed sex, too. It should not be treated like a gift that you give to your man if he's a good little boy or something that you withhold if he misbehaves. Sex is meant to be equally shared, not given as a birthday gift or negotiated like some sort of hostage situation.

*Love Note: You can, however, keep it spicy with fun games or bets, like "If Jake is the next Bachelor, you can (insert something kinky)." Oops! Freudian slip!*

## Don't #5—Ignore Issues

If there is something wrong in your relationship, sweeping it under the rug will only make it worse. That rug will eventually get so full of dirt and bumpy that you'll trip on it, fall really hard, and smash your pretty face.

*Love Note: Hot Chicks are not afraid to ask for help. If your relationship is troubled and you're really suffering, seek counseling or advice from a wise friend. Your love is worth fighting for, and even if you lose in the end, you will be able to rest easy knowing that you really tried.*

# Is It a Bust or a Blockbuster?

Now that you know the basics of acting like a Hot Chick in your relationship, we want to move on and make sure that your relationship itself is healthy and strong. We know how hard it is, but you need to end a relationship if it's not serving you, no matter how comfortable it may be. Since all relationships have their share of troubles, it can be hard sometimes to tell the difference between what's normal and what's not. How do you know when you're just going through a rough patch and when it's time to call it quits? Well, we're going to paint the picture in some hypothetical love scenes so that you can see if your love story is destined to be a total bust or a sizzling blockbuster. Is your relationship on track for a "Happy Ending," does it just need a little work so that you can have a beautiful "Take Two," or is it time to say, "Cut" and move on to a different love story? Take a look at these scenes and see how your love plays out.

***Love Scene #1:*** You and your lover get into a giant fight about sex, which turns into a fight about money, which turns into a fight about the piles of bills and dirty laundry. He says mean things that make you cry into your pillow feeling alone and totally confused.

*Happy Ending:* The next morning, he comes to you first thing with your favorite chocolate chip muffin and a giant apology. He feels terrible about what happened and agrees that you two need to work out these issues so that you can get back to loving each other.

*Take Two:* You would have liked more of an actual apology, but he does feel remorseful about the fight itself, and the two of you agree (again) to try and stop fighting.

*Cut:* He does not apologize for hurting your feelings or take any responsibility for the issues in your relationship. He's not willing to communicate with you or even talk about it. Instead, he goes out drinking with his friends and acts reckless or gives you the silent treatment and dirty looks for a week.

**Love Scene #2:** Instead of spending Saturday night with your lover, you decide to go out with the girls. It's Hot Chicks' night out, and you are looking hot as hell and are excited to hit the town with your BFFs!

*Happy Ending:* Your man tells you that you look gorgeous and asks you to check in with him if you're going to be out later than usual so that he doesn't worry. He gives you a kiss and tells you to be safe and have fun.

*Take Two:* He makes a comment about your skirt being short and says to be careful around your friend Marcy because she's "kind of a slut," but he kisses you before you leave and tells you to have a good time.

*Cut:* He tells you that you need to change because he doesn't want you going out with "your boobs hanging out." You get in a huge fight about it that spirals out of control and you end up making an excuse and not going out because you decide it's not worth making him so mad. Secretly, you know he's happy that he sabotaged your night out because this kind of thing happens often.

**Love Scene #3:** His ex-girlfriend calls him all the time. She's clearly not over him, and it's starting to cause problems in your relationship. This time, she calls in the middle of your anniversary dinner. What does he do?

*Happy Ending:* He doesn't answer her call and is honest with you about who it was. He focuses on you and your celebration for the rest of the night, and in the morning he sends her a text that says, "Please stop bothering me. I am trying to focus on my new relationship and you are fucking it up.♥"

*Take Two:* He answers the call and listens for a minute to what she's yapping about. He tells her that he can't talk now, hangs up, apologizes, and at least agrees not to take her calls in the middle of dinner but he isn't ready to cut off all communication.

*Cut:* He excuses himself and talks to her for fifteen minutes outside. When he comes back in he says, "She's my friend whether you like it or not, so you might as well stop being so insecure and jealous."

**Love Scene #4:** He goes out with his friends a lot, which only bothers you because you worry about him when it's late and/or he's drunk. You sit him down and tell him that checking in with you and promising to never, ever drive drunk would make you so much happier and less worried.

*Happy Ending:* He listens and tells you that he will try to do better and then he actually does. He makes a habit of texting you before leaving the bar, and calls for a ride if he's had a six pack and three tequila shots.

*Take Two:* He takes your concerns seriously enough to make an effort, but he often forgets to check in and you still worry. However, you've noticed that he's not driving drunk anymore, which is the most important improvement.

*Cut:* He cuts you off mid-conversation and tells you to stop being such a nervous Nellie. He says, "It's not my fault that you're such a worrywart," and insists that he shouldn't have to change his behavior just to make you happy.

**Love Scene #5:** He knows how important your family is to you and you've asked him to make an effort to get to know and love your family like his own.

*Happy Ending:* He invites your brother out for a beer and bites his tongue at your dad's insane political views. When you bitch and complain about your mom and your sister, he actually listens instead of egging you on or jumping on the shit-talking bandwagon.

*Take Two:* He makes an effort, but things like splitting holidays and spending money on your brother's bachelor party are hard for him. Sometimes he sides with your mom when you argue with her, but you figure that at least that means he's trying to get on your mom's good side!

*Cut:* He's not willing to compromise on the holidays, and so you end up spending most holidays apart. When he does spend time with your family, he always manages to bring up sensitive issues like money or religion, and when you get in a fight with your dad, he says, "That's no surprise; your dad is a moron."

# Love throughout Your Life

If that last section helped you recognize that your relationship either needs help or isn't worth saving, stay calm and know that you deserve to fix it or to move on and find a love that will serve you better. Not only do you deserve it, but you are capable of doing it. You are strong and beautiful and you mustn't settle for anything that isn't positive and healthy. Love takes bravery, whether it's the confidence to share your heart fully, the strength to fight for a love that's faltering, or the courage to end a relationship and strike out on your own. Being single takes bravery, too, to face spiders, holiday parties, and necklace clasps alone, but no matter what your relationship status is, we want you to have the courage to keep love in your heart and to spread love throughout your life.

We're not just talking about romantic love here, but treating everyone and everything in your life with love. When your boss is driving you crazy with her demands, keep love in your heart and remember that she's human, too. If your friend is going through a hard time, shower her with love and empathy. Perhaps most importantly, never forget to love yourself! Make nurturing and caring for yourself a top priority and never, ever tear yourself down or start to believe that you don't deserve all of the love in the world. When life is chaotic and you're feeling grumpy, fat, and OWL♥, work is stressful and your family is pissing you off, the love in your life is the only thing that will make you smile. And when tragedy strikes, it's the love that you put out into the universe♥ that will help you get out of bed and face whatever is going on in your life.

Love is like gasoline for life. If you keep your tank full, you will always be able to enjoy the ride, but if you let that needle hover around the red line, your soul can start to feel just as empty. Since we're in the mood for similes, love is also like a boomerang. If you put it out there, you will always get it back. In order to receive love, you have to give it out, so whether it means moving on from a relationship that's run its course with a heart full of love for yourself and respect for the relationship that once was, looking for love with the bravery to never settle, or keeping a relationship vibrant with constant TLC, get used to giving love out freely so that you can keep on getting it back.

# *Live It!*

We want to remind you one more time that you are a Hot Chick who deserves absolutely everything that life has to offer. You have the power burning in your hot body to change the way you feel about yourself, the track your career is on, and the amount of fun and love that you have in your life, and now you can rest easy knowing that you have the tools to transform your life into the life of your dreams.

No matter what setbacks you may have encountered in your life, nothing can truly hold you back but yourself. In order to be the best, brightest Hot Chick that you can be, you must be on a constant mission to spot your LSE♥ when it rears its ugly head and squash it like you're playing a killer game of whack-a-mole. Keep on telling yourself that you are not only a Hot Chick, but an intelligent, powerful, perfect, and beautiful woman. Do whatever you need to do to remember that, whether that means taping messages around your house or picking up this book and rereading the definition of a Hot Chick over and over again. Not only *can* you be her, but you already *are* her. You just need to start embracing it and acting like it in every part of your life.

It is time (right now!) to stop letting LSE♥, fear, OWL Syndrome♥, or a bad attitude rule your life and to instead choose to live your life like a Hot Chick. This is your one life and you can live it any way you want, but we hope you will choose to live it with excitement, inspiration, joy, and confidence. Even better, we know you can. Life is tough, ladies, and we are fighting the same battles as you—struggling with the same self-doubt, insecurities, bills, root canals, fights with our men, anxiety, stress, and moments of helplessness. We want to help you through it as we help each other, and we hope you'll help us by paying it forward and sharing our definition of a Hot Chick with other women and by boosting them up instead of tearing them down. Fill your life with confidence, savvy, meaningful work, an unforgettable heyday♥, celebrations, and love, and you will wake up one day feeling something wonderful . . . balance.

**We love you, Hot Chicks!**
**xoxo, Jodi & Cerina**

# Glossary

## Hot Lingo

**BMS:**
This stands for Bill Merrit Syndrome. Bill Merrit is one totally gross guy we dated, but he shares an affliction with many men who also suffer from BMS. The primary symptom is when a man uses his busy, important work schedule as an excuse to shut out the possibility of love or a relationship, or even some fun, crazy, messy sex. Secondary symptoms include being totally LSE♥ about sex and being stingy with compliments. Men with this syndrome tend to keep their balls in their briefcases, or else they just leave them in their desk drawers and only put them on at the office. Hot Chicks do not date men with BMS.

**Butt Class:**
You may not believe us, but we used to have a lame, flat, white-girl ass until we got that flat ass to the gym and started taking lots of butt classes! Butt classes are also called boring things like body sculpting or weight training, but we think our term is more

descriptive. Anyway, just like the Build-A-Bear Workshop that they have now and the Build-A-Boyfriend Workshop in *How to Love Like a Hot Chick*, this is like a Build-A-Butt Workshop. Butt classes include tons of squats, dead lifts, and lunges, and we prescribe taking them twice a week for maximum perky-butt benefits.

**Fantasy Sequence:**
A daydream that you purposely create, or one that just sort of happens when something or someone is in the back of your mind—your imagination runs wild and creates something totally fun. For example, you may have fantasy sequences about finally telling off that annoying chick at work who reads your emails over your shoulder, making out with your boyfriend in the middle of a boring meeting, or maybe just looking absolutely adorable and irresistible as you flirt with the hot barista at Starbucks.

**Foonge Face:**
Stems from the Italian spelling of fungi, meaning mushroom. If you look at a mushroom, the top of it curves down, looking like a little sad face. ☹ Girls with foonge faces feel sorry for themselves for no reason and walk around with grumpy looks on their faces. We encourage all you Hot Chicks to smile, knowing that you have the power to change your mood along with your reaction to anything that would give you a pouty little foonge face.

**Fucked Up:**
In our first book, we defined certain foods as being fucked up, and in our second book, we used this term for something in your love life that makes you feel LSE♥, scared, miserable, extremely jealous, passionless, untrusting, or furious. In this book, we are using this term to describe anything in your life that keeps you feeling unbalanced, insane, LSE♥, or that makes you suffer from OWL

Syndrome ♥. You might fuck up, your job might be fucked up, and any part of your life might be fucked up, but you need to deal with all of your fucked up shit in order to truly live like a Hot Chick.

**The Golden Rule:**

"Do onto others as you would want done onto you," or, "Love thy neighbor as thyself." There are a million different wordings for the golden rule, but they all mean the same thing: *treat other people exactly how you would want them to treat you in the same situation.* Living by the Golden Rule is a key Hot Chick trait because it means that you are honest and thoughtful and compassionate in every part of your life.

**Heyday:**

The very best, most magical, hottest time of your life—no matter what age box you check, or whether you're married or single, gay or straight. Your heyday begins when you stop having a pity party and decide that you're hot and worth all the fun in the world. You will look back one day and shake your head and giggle, remembering all of the fun, crazy, ridiculous times you had during your heyday. And it will be worth it.

**Heydayish:**

Our code word for when we're in the mood for some loving. Hot Chicks don't use the word horny, and there aren't many other good options to describe this feeling, either. We're feeling heydayish when we really, really want a big, giant boy to go downtown and then bake in our bed. Examples for using it in a sentence: "I only went home with him because I've been feeling heydayish," or, "I'm not going out tonight because I am feeling heydayish, and I might do something stupid."

**LBS:**

Stands for low blood sugar. LBS is a very serious condition, even for those of us without any medical problems. The symptoms of LBS are almost identical to those of another affliction we Hot Chicks suffer from, PMS. If we go too long without food, we become snarky, miserable, and downright inconsolable. Make sure to take care of yourself and eat every few hours, or the snapping, bitching, and fighting caused by your LBS is likely to wreak havoc on your relationships.

**LSE:**

Stands for Low Self Esteem. It is a disease that infects everyone from time to time, but Hot Chicks try really hard to cure themselves of this plague. The best thing about the term LSE is that it can be used as a noun, verb, adjective, or whatever. For example, you can be feeling LSE, someone can just be LSE, or your LSE can just act up unexpectedly. LSE is NOT hot, ladies, and recovering from this deadly infection is the first and biggest step to truly being a Hot Chick.

**Magic:**

This is our word for something or someone that is perfectly hot, is perfectly fun, or makes you feel like the happiest girl on the planet. Example for using it in a sentence: "I'm wearing my magic pants tonight," "Was your date magic?" or, "Something happened, our trip was magical!"

**OWL Syndrome:**

Stands for Overwhelmed With Life and is pronounced like the bird. OWL Syndrome can occur when you have way too much going on all at once, or if something unexpected happens (whether it's good or bad) that totally freaks you out. Example: OWL Syndrome can take effect when your boss puts a giant folder on your desk filled with crap that she wants you to finish by 6 p.m., you get a nasty, passive-aggressive email from your mother, and then that cute guy you met online calls to say he wants to have dinner with you tonight at 7.

## Play Small:

The origins of this term are actually from a Marianne Williamson quote—"Your playing small does not serve the world. There's nothing enlightening about shrinking so that others feel secure around you." We couldn't have said it better ourselves. Hot Chicks do not play small, apologize for who we are, or act LSE♥ to make people feel better about themselves. That's not hot, and to stop playing small is a big step toward living like a Hot Chick.

## Red Flags:

These are warning signs—sometimes they are gigantic and sometimes they're very subtle. Examples: A guy you're dating says to you, "I would tell you that you're beautiful, but I'm sure you hear that all the time." A little red flag should go up. This guy probably has BMS♥. Or how about when a superior in your business invites you to coffee to talk about future projects, and then "coffee" mysteriously turns into a candlelight dinner where he orders beef Carpaccio, opens a bottle of expensive vino, and buys you a rose? A GIANT red flag should go up, telling you that he doesn't want you involved in his business plan; he wants you naked in his bed.

## Self-Destructive Fantasy Sequences:

These are the negative, nasty versions of fantasy sequences♥. This is when your mind latches onto something horrific and upsetting and your imagination runs wild with it. It is not hot to indulge in these obnoxious thoughts! Don't let self-destructive fantasy sequences happen. You are only wasting precious time and energy that could be used towards your heyday ♥.

**Twitterpated:**
To be giddy and so overjoyed and anxious with feelings of love that it makes your heart pop out of your eyes whenever you're around your new crush. Origins—Disney's *Bambi*, when all the little animals were mating and falling in love because it was spring. Examples for using it in a sentence: "I know he's the one because it's been a year and a half and I'm still twitterpated," or, "I really didn't mean to have sex with him on the first date, but I couldn't help it, I was so twitterpated!"

**Universe:**
The universe is a stand-in for G*d or fate or whatever you believe in. The Hot Chicks believe firmly that the universe loves us and takes care of us and gives us exactly what we need in its proper time. But we have a give and take relationship with the universe—we have to tell it what we want and prepare ourselves so that we're ready when we get it. It's also important not to put bad things out into the universe. Examples for use in a sentence: "I keep getting hit on by creepy guys—I must be sending out a weird vibe and confusing the universe," or, "I feel good about that job interview. I did my best, and now it's up to the universe."

# Acknowledgments

**From Both of Us:**
A million thanks to our agent, Dan Mandel, for always support-
ing, believing in, and laughing with us; to the entire team at
HarperCollins, especially Emily Krump, Teresa Brady, Jen Hart,
Mary Ellen O'Neill, Carrie Kania, and everyone else who worked
so hard behind the scenes to bring this book to life; to Brad Petri-
gala for supporting us; and to Anne Cole for bringing us into the
HarperCollins family and believing in us from the start.

**From Jodi:**
I am so lucky to have been born into a family that has always
made me feel confident and capable of anything I set my mind to,
supported me in every endeavor, and is a complete blast to spend
time with, and to have married into one that is equally supportive
and fun. Endless thanks to both families, especially my amazing
parents and in-laws for providing so much love, guidance, and
laughter. There have been a few women in my life who taught me
everything I know about working like a Hot Chick; thank you to
Barbara Hogenson and Emily Bestler for being true inspirations,
and to Kimberly Whalen for believing in me. When it comes to
fun, I have to thank all of my friends in NY and LA, but especially
Robin Fineman and the late Sherie Weinstein, who truly knew
how to celebrate life better than anyone I've ever known. Cerina,
thank you for making work feel more like fun and fun feel even
more like fun; I have learned so much from you about balance
and am eternally grateful for our friendship. Finally, Dan, thank
you for being the thing that makes everything else worthwhile. I
love you.

**From Cerina:**

Thank you to my Hot Chick momma who I love dearly. You wear more hats than I would know what to do with, always manage to balance your stress with grace, and still have room in your life for martinis and sundaes. Dad, I love you and thank you for continuing to teach me to "stop and smell the roses." I hold that near and dear to my heart and that is precisely what this book is about. Gino and Angela, I love you more than air, our relationships give me peace, and it's truly amazing to see you both live such incredible, full lives. Steve, the world's best father-in-law and president of my HMB fan club, thank you for your love and support. A giant thanks to all my beautiful, successful Hot Chick girlfriends who keep my life full of magic♥ moments: Courtney, Karen, Toni, Nicole, Lisa, and Krista . . . what in the world would I do without you? Elisa—our burgers and wine give me strength and sanity, Mandy, it's your turn twin cuz—I love you and look up to you. And thank you, Jodi, the best biz partner and BFF *ever*— from heyday♥ moments with way too much topping to our lovely yet crazy lives now, with every word we write I love you more deeply and I feel blessed moving through life with such a Hot Chick by my side. And Bennie, darling, thanks for having a glass of wine (or two) with me at the end of long, hard, stressful days; letting me watch CNN; and when business makes me OWL♥, for making me feel like life is loving, sane, exciting, hot and perfectly balanced.

# MORE FROM
# JODI LIPPER & CERINA VINCENT

## HOW TO EAT LIKE A HOT CHICK
### Eat What You Love, Love How You Feel

ISBN 978-0-06-156086-6 (paperback)

With sassy wit and good will to spare, Jodi and Cerina reveal their tricks to overcoming any food obstacle, from which cocktails will keep you light on your feet well past midnight, to how to stay on track if you're down in the dumps (or if you just got dumped).

## HOW TO LOVE LIKE A HOT CHICK
### The Girlfriend to Girlfriend Guide to Getting the Love You Deserve

ISBN 978-0-06-170644-8 (paperback)

Jodi and Cerina tutor readers through all phases of relationships, from the little-known joys of being single, to first, second, and third dates, falling in love, and all the way through marriage. Each chapter includes Hot Chick rules for every scenario (and permission to break those rules when the situation calls for it).

## LIVE LIKE A HOT CHICK
### How to Feel Sexy, Find Confidence, and Create Balance at Work and Play

ISBN 978-0-06-195907-3 (paperback)

Jodi and Cerina are out to wake up your inner Hot Chick so that you can make the most of every day by creating balance, being confident, and taking charge of your life.